THE ATTITUDES OF A CHAMPION

THE WARRIOR WITHIN

VICTOR COLEMAN SR.

CONTENTS

INTRODUCTION

What is a champion? How important is a champion's attitude? These are two questions that must be answered by everyone who wants to live victoriously.

I want you to take the time to jot down your answer to these questions before taking this journey. What you find in the pages of this book will challenge you to discover the importance of attitude in succeeding in any area of your life.

I have learned that my attitude impacts me more than it impacts others. Understanding who I am and who God made me to be keeps me focused and gives me peace. When I learned what being a champion is all about, that lesson keeps me humble and ready to take on whatever life brings.

Champions come in many forms and just as many attitudes can be found in each. Let's take, for example, the story of David and Goliath. Both men were champions, each with their own style and way of doing things. Each had a different attitude. Both had their own perception about what they were facing. Like them, you must understand you are created to be a champion, but your attitude may determine your success. Let's explore more.

"4 Then Goliath, a Philistine champion from Gath, came out of the

Philistine ranks to face the forces of Israel. He was over nine feet tall!" 1 Samuel 17:4 (NLT)

The keyword "Champion" is one of the most appealing terms in the Bible. The King James Bible Dictionary defines a champion as someone who undertakes combat in the place or cause of another or someone who fights in his own cause. A champion is described as someone who wins despite the odds.

People seek ways to always demonstrate the traits of a champion. Those traits, however, may not always be visible. This book takes a more intentional and spirit-led approach to bringing to light the traits and attitudes of a champion from the perspective of God's Word.

This book aims at teaching and inspiring you through biblical references on the attitudes of a champion so you can discover how to harness all that potential as you represent Christ on Earth. In this book, you will unravel the top attitudes of a champion that cut across varying virtues and how you can maximize them for long term impact.

We know that a champion is a warrior, thus the subtitle "The Warrior Within." A warrior is a fighter. Warriors are traditionally trained to fight and defeat their enemies. They specialize in combat or warfare. They must be skilled in the strategy of warfare and excellent in using all manner of weapons of combat.

In each of us, we are expected to have a "warrior's attitude." To get this attitude, you must retrain the way you see everything. When I was in the military, we were all taught to approach every situation from a soldier's perspective. They trained us to operate in multiple environments, cultures and situations. This training was to teach us to adapt to the situation. Therefore, the warrior in you must be prepared for all situations. Our fight isn't against flesh and blood, therefore, we must be ready to go to war against our enemy. If you are going to come out a victor from every battle, you must be thoroughly trained. Your attitude, temperament and mind must be developed to be able to be calm and focused in every situation.

Warriors know the strategies of their opponents. They are aware of the tricks and distractions that would cause them to be unable to concentrate on what they really should be fighting. Warriors are trained so they aren't preoccupied, diverted or flustered by their enemies' ploys. For example, we can be distracted from exhibiting love by not fully forgiving others. This will cause us to fail the test and lose out. Look at the following scriptures:

"9 For this was my purpose in writing, to see if you would stand the test, whether you are obedient and committed to following my instruction in all things. 10 If you forgive anyone anything, I too forgive [that one]; and what I have forgiven, if I have forgiven anything, has been for your sake in the presence of [and with the approval of] Christ, 11 to keep Satan from taking advantage of us; for we are not ignorant of his schemes." I Cor 2:11 (AMP)

Notice Paul says there is a place we can be where the enemy can take advantage of us. One of those places is unforgiveness. If we are trained warriors, we can have victory. Victory only comes when we are not ignorant of the Devil's strategies.

It is important to know how the "Goliaths" of our lives can distract us if we haven't been instructed in identifying "his" strategy. Paul wrote that the church of Corinth would pass the test by being obedient and committed to following instructions. You will have victory as you obey instructions.

In the Bible, Goliath was a champion. Just because he was on the other side did not make his victories less important than anyone else. Goliath was bold and probably intimidating to listen to. The text describes his height and the armor he wore. I can imagine the size and details of his helmet and how they were fashioned to be intimidating.

Goliath's taunt was that of confidence and boldness. He insulted the army of God and did not have respect for them. He said things that would make someone mad and fight or become afraid and do nothing. As a "champion," Goliath did what he was supposed to do. He used his past victories to speak boldly. He used his voice to intimidate his foes. He is like people you know who seem to be "champions" without being humble.

Many, however, will not tap into true greatness as Goliath did. If Goliath could tap into his greatness without God, what can be done by someone who has God? Let me encourage you today to tap into the power of God that is in you.

The only way you are going to tap into God's power is through a relationship with God and prayer. The center of all the principles of the book is the belief you must have a consistent and effective prayer life. Prayer is not what you occasionally do, it must be your lifestyle. Each attitude must be developed with the study of God's Word and prayer. Make up your mind that prayer will be your mantle.

This book isn't for everyone. It is only for those who want to get unstuck. It is only for those who are tired of talking about what they are going to do and are ready to move forward. If you aren't one of these people, don't waste time reading this book. You cannot move forward until you act. You can't keep making promises to win without developing a winner's attitude. You have waited and waited, and nothing has happened. You have prayed and prayed, and nothing has changed. It is time to pick up your mat and walk. In other words: act.

Within the pages of this book, we will pull out secrets to being champions. We will discuss what makes them win. We will explore what makes leaders and champions do big things in the face of significant opposition. We will look at attitudes that heroes possess and discover ways to appropriate those attributes.

Champions for the Lord acquire and maintain strong character qualities. Each of those qualities is necessary for us to have victory in every area of our lives. We win at home, work, or on the field because of our godly characteristics. We understand that once the labour is complete, there are rewards. David killing Goliath positioned him to have favour with the king and with men and it also gave him opportunities for greater rewards and eventually led to him becoming king.

There is a warrior within that is waiting to do mighty things. Stay focused on developing these attitudes and you will receive rewards fitting a champion. Like David, you need to invest time in learning and developing these attributes of a winner, and that is why this book is so timely. Instead of listing the attitudes and telling you what they can do in your life, I will guide and show you how to learn them so that you win in EVERY area of your life.

David started to win as a shepherd, a little boy who only knew how to tend to his father's flock. He took that winning streak from the farm to the palace. You can do the same as David. You can utilize the attitudes of a champion to win in the smallest and biggest aspects of your life.

Are you ready to put in the work and get started? We will commence our journey with a champions' first attitude, which reveals a lot of their personality. Champions must overcome their inability to see beyond their problems.

Please take your time to read the scripture verses first before reading the chapter's content, as this will help you maintain a connection with God's Word as you read. Let us begin with some inspiration from 1 Samuel 17.

1

CHAMPIONS SEE BEYOND THE PROBLEM

YOU WILL FACE PROBLEMS. You will face a Goliath. You will have problems that speak to you loud and clear. Can you see the problem you're faced with and understand it is not greater or bigger than God? Can you see yourself conquering the Goliaths around you? Warriors are trained to believe they are better than their opponents.

> *"26 David asked the soldiers standing nearby, 'What will a man get for killing this Philistine and ending his defiance of Israel? Who is this pagan Philistine anyway, that he is allowed to defy the armies of the living God?'" 1 Samuel 17:26 (NLT)*

The first idea to attribute to a champion is that they often view things differently than others, and this is a crucial concept that sets them apart from others. Where others see problems, champions see opportunities. David is an excellent example of how heroes see things differently. Let's look at 1 Samuel 17:10-11;32-37 (NLT)

> *"10 'I defy the armies of Israel today! Send me a man who will fight me!' 11 When Saul and the Israelites heard this, they were terrified and deeply shaken."*

> *"32 'Don't worry about this Philistine,' David told Saul. 'I'll go fight him!' 33 "Don't be ridiculous!' Saul replied. 'There's no way you can fight this Philistine and possibly win! You're only a boy, and he's been a man of war since his youth.' 34 But David persisted. 'I have been taking care of my father's sheep and goats,' he said. 'When a lion or a bear comes to steal a lamb from the flock, 35 I go after it with a club and rescue the lamb from its mouth. If the animal turns on me, I catch it by the jaw and club it to death. 36 I have done this to both lions and bears, and I'll do it to this pagan Philistine, too, for he has defied the armies of the living God! 37 The Lord who rescued me from the claws of the lion and the bear will rescue me from this Philistine!'" (NLT)*

In the situation described above, Saul, the Israelites, and the armies of Israel heard words of fear from Goliath and became terrified and shaken. Now the text says in verse 10 that Goliath shouted. Everyone heard the same thing and responded differently than David.

What makes you rise above what you are facing? Let's look at the facts. David heard Goliath say the same words, but he saw something different. Goliath's words didn't affect him as they did with the Israelites. Why?

Goliath threatened them for 40 days. Within that time frame, he may or may not have been there to hear it. But what we can determine is that David's faith did not waver during the situation. To get this type of faith, you must have experience.

David was a self-described champion. He gave his testimony about what he had done and what he could do. He didn't see defeat because he was focused on his victories.

Champions do not see defeat even when others might believe it.

They press on and fight for what they believe based on what they know.

It is not easy being a champion, especially if you have the wrong perspective about life. What set David apart was his perspective of God and the children of Israel were God's army. His belief and attitude helped him win mentally first before dealing with Goliath physically. Like David, you must see yourself and your team as belonging to God. The enemy will appear menacing like Goliath. Big, threatening, and even better equipped, but if you see like the rest of the team does, fear will become a comfortable companion.

I encourage you today to look at whatever is opposing you as though it was going against God. When you look at things from God's point of view, you will have the determination and commitment to never give up, never give in, never back up, never back down, never sit down, never quit and never walk away until victory is achieved. God has given us the heart of champions. Much like a good Earthly father, God wants his children to win in whatever they do.

Our Heavenly Father desires that we win in life, but that is HIS desire. We also must believe that the desire can come to fruition, and this is why we must become proactive with seeing things differently. We must be champions in the areas of our lives where we've been given a vision, a goal, a dream, or a calling.

We must prevail as champions over the areas where we've been given stewardship because it is in those areas, small or big, we can start to build inner resilience and foster the traits that lead to a "victor's attitude." How else could the little David stand confidently and speak to Goliath without fear? David gained such confidence by focusing on his victories and not so much on the problem.

If you only see obstacles and challenges as things that will defeat you and/or your team, you will never find solutions or see victory. God has given us a tool that enables transformation, and it is called the mind. Start by equipping and empowering your mind with God-like thinking by studying scriptures daily and other material relating to what you want.

It may take time for you to change all you believed in and alter your perspective, but as we progress on this journey, you will begin to

experience a much needed paradigm shift. Godly champions see differently because they get their truth from God and hold on to their faith.

Building on what we've learned thus far, we will unravel another
champion's attitude which focuses on the question: How are they
committed to rising above and dealing with bullying and pressure?
Let's find the answers.

CHAMPIONS RISE ABOVE INTIMIDATION

You must confront to conquer.

— VICTOR COLEMAN

"**4** *Then Goliath, a Philistine champion from Gath, came out of the Philistine ranks to face the forces of Israel. He was over nine feet tall!* **5** *He wore a bronze helmet, and his bronze coat of mail weighed 125 pounds.* **6** *He also wore bronze leg armor, and he carried a bronze javelin on his shoulder.* **7** *The shaft of his spear was as heavy and thick as a weaver's beam, tipped with an iron spearhead that weighed 15 pounds. His armor bearer walked ahead of him carrying a shield.* **8** *Goliath stood and shouted a taunt across to the Israelites. "Why are you all coming out to fight?" he called. "I am the Philistine champion, but you are only the servants of Saul. Choose one man to come down here and fight me!" 1 Sam 17:4-8 (NLT)*

INTIMIDATION IS the hallmark trait of any combatant. Intimidation comes through people and life situations. Whether we are intimidated by a person or test, we must understand we can conquer it. This will never happen, however, if we do not confront our issue.

As you can see, Goliath's first strategy was to intimidate the Israelites with frightful words and bully them into surrendering. Did you notice the keywords in the verse? Words like, "Shouted," "Fight," "Heavy," "Thick," and "Armor." Did you notice the description of Goliath, that his words and his armor were frightening? These are words and physical attributes that bring pressure to discourage you from" thinking about" winning. However, champions do not let those things stop them. You must commit yourself to rise above all forms of pressure, bullying, and extortion that are used to deflate your spirit. The people of Israel stood by and listened to Goliath defy God, mock Saul and their army for 40 days. How long have you watched, listened to, or carried images or thoughts that taunt you? People like David don't listen to negative taunts for that long without doing something.

Why didn't they stand up to the intimidation? Why didn't they do something to free themselves from that situation? Well, they didn't because they were afraid and intimidated. But do you know what God doesn't do? He doesn't tolerate intimidation, and he doesn't threaten people. You also shouldn't tolerate bullying nor intimidate others.

Intimidation must be met with confidence and reliance on the Holy Spirit. II Timothy 1:7,: *"For the Holy Spirit, God's gift, does not want you to be afraid of people, but to be wise and strong, and to love them and enjoy being with them." (TLB)*

Intimidation is a tool used by the Devil to cause you to doubt yourself and feel overwhelmed by life's challenges. This leads to deflating your faith and the reason for not using your faith. There are two things to remember in this chapter. The first is how you can avoid the "Average" mentality, and the second is how you can focus on what you have.

1. DEFEATING WRONG THINKING: SITUATIONS AND ISSUES CAN EASILY TERRORIZE ORDINARY PEOPLE

The first idea is that ordinary people can be easily terrorized by the situations and issues they face. But you are not ordinary or "Average" and you shouldn't allow such mediocrity in your life. You must learn how to defeat wrong thinking. You can do all things through Christ only if you believe it. Intimidation comes when you aren't sure and that comes from lack of knowledge. People with wrong thinking don't rise above intimidation, champions do. Let's go back to the verse in 1 Samuel to figure out why changing our thinking is essential to rise above intimidation.

In the text, notice that Goliath came from the ranks of his army to taunt. Remember, what intimidates you can be singled out. Goliath was so confident that he left his team and stood out in the open with his massive armor and armor barrier. The things you single out and make big will cause you to lose focus and perspective. It also might have you believe a lie more than the truth. For example, just because you get laid off, doesn't mean you are going to lose your house. You must break the habit of overthinking or underthinking a problem. Yes, these are habits. Any habit you don't confront, you will not conquer.

David didn't focus on what Goliath was wearing or saying, he focused on the truth of defeating a lion and bear by the hands of God. Champions rise above the noise and think of victory.

The Bible gives such descriptive details as proof that there were important details to the story. The children of Israel were facing a cocky opponent who had followers. When you focus on your "Goliath" and everything that seems to be supporting it, it can discourage you. Therefore, it is important not to focus on the other distractors. When you feel intimidated, often it is not just one thing you are thinking about. Champions learn how to pick apart their problems.

Wrong thinking people can't prioritize what is important. Sure, the Philistine army was important, but they weren't as intimidating as Goliath. He was the one doing the taunting. There was a Philistine army, but Goliath was the elephant in the room.

Goliath was huge and intimidating, but he wasn't bigger than God. Focusing on the "Big" thing may cause many to fear and lose perspective. For example, don't focus on what people have and what you may be missing out on, else you will become discouraged, especially if what they have is perceived as better than yours. These thoughts will taunt and terrorize you.

Think about this: Goliath was thought to be more significant than David and more experienced in traditional warfare than David. Also, Goliath's gear was better than David's sling and rocks. None of that discouraged David. What if David would have focused on this? It would have discouraged him. David knew what he had to do to win, and this reduced Goliath's intimidation tactics to work on him.

To defeat average thinking, you must renew your mind and to look at situations from different angles. As David looks through the lens of God to diminish the thoughts of what he was seeing in the natural, so should you. Defeating bad thinking requires constant reinforcement of positive and victorious thoughts. Thoughts such as, "more than a conqueror," or, "I can do all things through Christ," or, "nothing shall harm me," are just a few that come to mind in defeating images or taunts that cause discouragement. You must keep playing victorious music and songs.

2. DEFEATING INTIMIDATION REQUIRES FOCUS: CHAMPIONS FOCUS ON WHAT THEY HAVE AND ARE CONFIDENT THEY CAN WIN

Secondly, champions always focus. Their focus is on what it will take them to win. They focus on what they have, what they can do, who is on their team and are greatly confident in their ability to win. From the moment David opened his mouth to speak, he exuded confidence because he had a champion's mentality.

The enemy will always show you something negative in the physical or in your mind to intimidate you and to take you off focus. For example, David's brother's comments could have been a distraction that could have taken his focus. Or Saul's armor could have been a distraction to cause David to lose focus. Maybe Goliath's experiences could have been a distraction point for David. However, neither caused him to lose focus.

Nehemiah was building a wall and others wanted him to come and entertain their complaint. However, he said, *"I am carrying on a great project and cannot go down. Why should the work stop while I leave it and go down to you?"* Nehemiah 6:3 (NIV) He refused to stop what he was doing and go "down" to them. Distractions cause us to go down. Stay focused on what is up.

You must identify and ignore anything that causes you to be distracted from the "great project" God has for you. You are on assignment and must carry on the work. Don't let history or things present or in the future cause you to be distracted in this season you are in.

*"For the Lord sees not as man sees: man looks on the
outward appearance, but the Lord looks on the heart."*
1 Samuel 16:7 (ESV)

Please stop looking at things and letting them paralyze you. God warns us about letting outward appearances influence our decisions. We must look deeper. If you look at what you don't have, you won't focus on what you do have. Do you know that God is on your side? What is in your heart? If you don't focus on that, other things will make you think you are defeated or will be defeated.

If David focused on the traditional armor and weaponry of that time and thought he would only have victory if he had it, too, he would have never entered battle. He didn't let those things (or lack thereof) intimidate him nor did he allow not having experience of war intimidate him. You need to know that bad attitudes look big and shout loud but they can't stop you.

Don't let your intimidators stop you. Your enemies shouldn't stop you from running races or succeeding in life. Intimidations are tools of the enemy that are used to make you believe you can't win.

Yes, by the way. Just like you need to know "not to go down," you also need to know when to go and fight. Sometimes you must go down and fight. Remember, Goliath said, "Come down here and fight me!" My opinion is, "If I am down, I might as well fight my way back up." Therefore, when your enemies shout and your only way to victory is going through the valley, go down and fight. The Lord is with you. Remember that, as a soldier of the Lord, you are above average and can destroy your enemies. You are not average. God doesn't do "average." You are above and not beneath. You are more than a conqueror. You are the head and not the tail. You are a world changer and giant slayer. You are beautifully and wonderfully created by God.

Speaking of average, remember God's opinion of the Church at Laodicea as seen in the book of Revelation (Rev 3:14-18). In God's letter to the Laodicea church, he had nothing good to say about them. As the scripture suggests, he pointed out that they were neither hot nor cold; they were average. This description means that they weren't good or bad, just average. God preferred to either be hot or cold than luke-warm (average). You are in the middle. But read this carefully: "When a person is average, they're as close to the bottom as they are to the top."

It is not sinful to be average. You can have an average income, an average job, or be an average athlete. God encourages us to excel in every area of our lives. He wants us to be successful and not just fake it. To excel beyond average, you must change the way you think.

Sadly, most people, including many believers, seek the tangible trappings of success but ignore what it means to be successful. This is because of thinking. You cannot be at the top until you genuinely break out from being average minded. To do this requires focusing on what is above and moving in that direction.

Wrong thinking can cause us to be like a dead fish, you can go with the flow. You are strong and made in the image of our Creator to swim in all currents.

Saul's army did nothing with the fact that God was on their side. Although they knew it, they were afraid. We need to make a quality commitment daily to confront intimidation. Confront what is intimi-dating you and become the best you can be in everything.

You can't defeat what you don't confront. Let's confront the enemy of intimidation by focusing our thoughts on who we are and actions on what needs to be defeated.

We confront things first in prayer. You will not be able to defeat anything without spending time with God and His word in focused prayer. Throughout David's life, you will find him talking to God. You must have an effective prayer life. You must seek the Lord to know who/what battles to fight, and when, how and where to fight those battles.

In summation, to defeat intimidation you must pray, take action, stay focused, face your fears, move forward, and strive to be above average. More importantly, know that you are made in God's image and nothing formed against you will succeed.

Well done! With attitude Number Two, you see how to combat intimidation and stand firm in God's Word. Now we will unravel attitude Number Three, which speaks of how champions have heart and what makes up the heart of a champion.

3

CHAMPIONS HAVE HEART

"Yet in all these things we are more than conquerors and gain an overwhelming victory through Him who loved us [so much that He died for us]." Romans 8:37 (AMP)

"People look at the outward appearance, but the Lord looks at the heart." 1 Samuel 16:7 (NIV)

HAVE you ever heard someone being described as "having heart?" If you have, you will agree with me that it means the person is someone with a good heart or someone that has "fight" in them. Since goodness comes from God, people who have such hearts are empowered by Him, and that is what you need to become a champion. It is God who put the fight in you. He calls us "Mighty men of Valor." Someone with valor is someone who has great courage in the time of battle. They have heart.

The definition of heart in the biological sense of the word is "the organ that controls the flow of blood in the body, or the center of human emotion." It controls your adrenaline and emotional fortitude. The heart controls whether we can run far or not at all. It can determine our motivation to get up or stay seated. It controls our mood.

This is why it is so important to guard our heart. Scripture says, *"Above all else, guard your heart, for everything you do flows from it."* Prov 4:23 (NIV) It says again, *"He is not afraid of bad news; his heart is firm, trusting in the Lord."* Psalm 112:7 (ESV)

Chuck Norris, the karate champion and movie star, said, "People come up to me and say, 'Chuck, you're the luckiest guy in the world to be a world karate champion and a movie and TV star.' When they say this to me, I kind of smile because luck had nothing to do with it; God had everything to do with it."

True champions know that God is their strength and leads them to victory. I always appreciate the saying that says, "Your life as you know it can change in an instant." Knowing that God is the source of my ability to have victory, I know at any moment my situation can change just as David's life changed when he confronted Goliath.

But David's transformation is attributed to what was in his heart. He knew deep within that he couldn't do it on his own. David possessed courage that his fellow Israealites didn't have. What is in your heart? Are you guarding or protecting it?

There are three lessons to learn from David about the heart of a champion. These lessons will give insight into how to develop the heart of a champion.

1. THE HEART OF A CHAMPION IS CONTROLLED BY CONVICTIONS

The Heart (mind) of a champion ensures their convictions are in alignment with their purpose. Their convictions cause them to rise above their circumstances.

David had convictions or resolve that this fight wasn't about land or an earthly kingdom, but about God's reputation. When faced with big problems, there must be a huge conviction driving you. This realization is necessary in rising to take on big tasks.

David was already extraordinary, but it would take a giant for his greatness to be seen by others. He takes on lions and bears: not an ordinary person. Who ignores the voices of a bully who is more significant and more experienced in war than they are? Not an average person. No, it takes someone who has something in their heart more significant than the problem they face.

2. THE HEART OF A CHAMPION IS CONTROLLED BY SOMETHING GREATER, SOMETHING EXTRAORDINARY

The mind of a champion understands that no problem is too difficult to be solved. They know when to see beyond the problem and embrace the possibilities. They look beyond the issue in front of them and imagine all the greatness that can unfold if they rely more on God for the victory, just like David did.

David had in his heart that there were rewards on the other side of victory. The king promised whoever killed the Philistine champion would be set for life. When you have other things driving you, it causes you to rise above ordinary and move you to do extraordinary things. While others are taking the traditional path of waiting for things to get better, you walk with the champion's mindset and step out and take actions.

3. THE HEART OF A CHAMPION IS CONTROLLED BY FAITH IN THEMSELVES

A champion must know that they will do the right thing when the time comes. She believes in herself because she knows God has given her what it takes to win.

Sugar Ray Robinson once said, *"To be a champion, you have to believe in yourself when no one else will."* David also said this when he faced Goliath, "I will fight Him." David had heart and wasn't afraid of the giant.

To become a champion, you must know that the only thing to do when the time comes is the right thing, even if you are in the minority. The Israelites were ready to give in and lose the war even without fighting because they lacked such a heart. But David being in the minority stood up for them against Goliath and said:

"Don't worry about the Philistines." David told Saul, "I'll go fight him!" He also said in verse 37, "The Lord who rescued me from the claws of the lion and the bear will rescue me from this Philistine." (NLT)

David's confidence was from his heart, a heart of God, and a heart emboldened by faith. Just like Sugar Ray said, for anyone to become a champion, he/she must believe in themselves. Have confidence in your abilities, and always believe in your God-given talents.

4. CHAMPIONS THINK VICTORY ALL THE TIME

David said, "The Lord will rescue and deliver me," because his mind had developed to trust in God. His confidence was rooted in God. He knew that God would destroy his enemy and use him to get it done. Having an attitude like this will reinforce your confidence for victory.

Look at the verses below and put them to memory:

Romans 8:37 says, *"Yet in all these things we are more than conquerors and gain an overwhelming victory through him who loved us [so much that He died for us]."* (AMP)

1 Corinthians 15:57 says, *"But thanks be to God, who gives us the victory [as conquerors through our Lord Jesus Christ]."* (AMP)

These scriptures encourage us and let us know that regardless of what happens, you have victory. When you make a decision, obstacles and problems will occur; however, you must not give up. You must not let situations or people talk you out of your decision to make progress. Saul tried to talk to discourage David engagement with Goliath, but David didn't listen because he believed he was more than a conqueror.

The heart controls you. Guard what goes in as well as maintain what is in there. A champion constantly evolves in the way they will defeat their opponent. They realize the solution needed for one victory may not be good for the next. They constantly renew their mind in order to be victorious each time. You must be resolute to build a heart filled with God's Word so that your faith is greater than your fears in any situation. In Chapter Four, we will talk about criticisms and how champions handle those moments.

4

CHAMPIONS IGNORE CRITICISM

"But when David's oldest brother, Eliab, heard David talking to the men, he was angry. 'What are you doing around here anyway?' he demanded. 'What about those few sheep you're supposed to be taking care of? I know about your pride and deceit. You just want to see the battle!'

"29 'What have I done now?' David replied. 'I was only asking a question!' 30 He walked over to some others and asked them the same thing and received the same answer. 31 Then David's question was reported to King Saul, and the King sent for him. 32 'Don't worry about this Philistine,' David told Saul. 'I'll go fight him!'" 1 Samuel 17: 28-32. (NLT)

CRITICISM IS a part of life's experiences because people will always have opinions about what you do and the steps you take. Everyone faces criticism because not everyone will agree on everything. The feeling from criticism has paralyzed some while causing others to act horrifically. It is through learning to handle your emotions we learn to have victory over critics.

David's brother could not see him as a champion. He saw him as prideful, arrogant, and deceitful. He criticizes him without David doing anything wrong; you may have similar feelings.

Before taking hasty steps towards reacting to the criticism, let's consider 1 Samuel Chapter 17:28:

> *"But when David's oldest brother, Eliab, heard David talking to the men, he was angry. 'What are you doing around here anyway?' he demanded. 'What about those few sheep you're supposed to be taking care of? I know about your pride and deceit. You just want to see the battle!'" (NLT)*

There are times in your life as a champion you must be ready to face your opponents. You will need to know how to manage angry people who criticize you. You will need to know how to handle having your motives questioned. Finally, you must be ready to ignore people belittling you and your current assignment.

Eliab was angry because David was asking questions. You will not be able to explain someone else's anger against you. You might think they are jealous or just haters. It doesn't matter why they are angry; don't spend time focusing on it. Leave it up to the Lord.

Next, you must anticipate that people are going to question your motives. Eliab thought David just wanted to "see the battle." It appeared that the Israelites were waiting to see what would happen, therefore, he thought David was there for that purpose. He didn't know the motive of David. Sometimes people will try to reflect their motives on you. You must stay focused and move with confidence toward your goal. Yes, sometimes you will ask questions for clarification. Don't get distracted trying to deal with others who try to figure out your motives without asking you. Don't fill your mind with your own information thinking for others and don't let them do it to you.

People will criticize what they don't understand and question why you are doing what you are doing. In other words, they will question your motives. Sometimes people who have bad motives think others are like them. If your motives are pure, don't waste time justifying them especially to someone who is already mad for no apparent reason.

Finally, you must know how to ignore people who belittle you and your work. Eliab trivilizes David's current assignment of keeping his father's sheep, "What about the few sheep you are supposed to be taking care of?" Are you just starting your business or assignment and someone has belittled your effort? Encourage yourself. You may have been laboring for a long time, and you have not seen the significant return on your investment of time and effort. Don't give up. Let me encourage you to keep going, especially if family and those closest to you can't see the champion you are because they are only looking at your past/present mistake and can't see your future.

1. CHAMPIONS HAVE THE GIFT TO IGNORE CRITICS

To ignore people sometimes must be seen as a gift. If you are doing something or you are thinking of doing something, expect critics. People are often comfortable with their mess, and some people would rather be safe than taking a chance of being embarrassed or failing. Face it, no one likes criticism. However, you must not let the voice of critics paralyze you just like David did not let Eliab's criticism paralyze him. Eliab was angry because David was talking to men about their enemy and he belittled David's current assignment in 1 Samuel 17:28: *"What about those few sheep you're supposed to be taking care of?"* (NLT)

Sometimes it is those close to you that will criticize your assignments, and sometimes people will not see you doing anything more significant than what you are doing. Sometimes people will say, "How are you going to do something bigger when you have so little?"

"What have I done now?" David replied. "I was only asking a question!" 1 Samuel 17:29 (NLT)

When David replied to his brother, he never addressed the criticism. He just told him what he was doing. The easiest way to ignore criticism is to leave them with a question. Tell them what you are doing (or did) if you must, but don't spend time entertaining their criticism.

Let's learn a few more things from David's attitude as a champion.

2. CHAMPIONS DON'T HOLD ONTO CRITICISMS

David didn't hold on to the blame. He ignored his brother because he was on his way to another God-ordained assignment and didn't need the distraction. God has a plan for you! When someone does not receive your gift, your gift will make room for you in someone else's kitchen. While others are trapped in cages of criticism, intimidation and fears, champions confront theirs. When others are bogged down entertaining critics, winners focus on what helps them to succeed.

When I was a project manager for the government, I managed a lot of large projects. I was also told that I didn't have the experience nor did my teams have the expertise. I was told people didn't want my projects done, and many executives and managers saw things we were doing as impossible tasks or not important.

But I learned that in order to win, I had to ignore the criticisms and keep my spirits up. I trusted God each time to give me victory, and He did. I believed nothing was too hard for God. It was keeping this mindset that protected me from the negative impact of criticism.

3. A CHAMPION'S CONVICTIONS OVERRIDE CRITICISMS

Sometimes others will not agree with you, be mad at you, and just not like you. Don't give up. Maintain your courage. You will need the prevailing "can do" attitude to push past the harsh words of naysayers and remain focused to defeat your enemies.

To get past criticism, you must have goals and purposes bigger than the voices of the criticism you will encounter. Your purpose and conviction must never be smaller than what your critics are shouting.

David had a "God will rescue me" conviction. That conviction overruled the taunts of Goliath and the fear of King Saul. Your beliefs should supersede your critics' voices. After all, every champion has critics. Walk out your convictions.

4. CHAMPIONS WALK AWAY FROM CRITICS

Winners don't have the time to allow the critics' words to discourage them from attaining their goals. Hence, they walk away from critics. David knew what he would do regardless of what his brother said. He took courage and walked away from Eliab. You can do the same thing, too.

No matter how someone mocks your assignment or questions your motives, you must know when to walk away. Don't hold onto what you know is not true. Don't stand there and listen to nonsense for "40 days." The scriptures tell us to, "hold on to the good." Negative talk is not good; so why are you holding it. Drop it. Because David didn't want to lose his opportunity, he didn't hold on to the criticism nor did he stick around listening to his brother. As soon as he walked and got aligned with the right people, his name and message got in the King's ear.

Champions don't spend time entertaining what others say about them, especially if the criticism is not valid or isn't constructive in reaching the goal. Winners keep it moving. They understand that sometimes people close to them often don't appreciate or see the best in them. They will only tell you what you can't do or make light of what you are doing. Others will question why you are doing something (motive), while some will misrepresent your character. If you are going to overcome this, you must find ways to ignore detractors without being angry or hard to get along with. You must know who you are and what you are capable of doing. Know the skills you possess because they will work for you. David had the gift of ignoring his critics, and you need that gift. He had the gift of walking away from those who didn't understand him. Is it time for you to walk? David ignored his brother and walked into his destiny. So the question is, "Will you walk into your season of victory?"

Don't get angry or upset when someone criticizes you, especially when you are confident about the assignment God has given you. Some may criticize you because they lack understanding of your vision, and it is your responsibility to prove how viable your dream is by winning just like David.

If you listen to critics too long, it may lead to fear or low esteem. We know that when fear is present, faith won't work properly. How do champions respond to fear? How do they ensure that negative talk will not lead to low self esteem. In Chapter Five you will understand why fear has no place in "the heart of a champion." Getting rid of fear lifts your esteem.

5

CHAMPIONS CONFRONT THEIR FEARS

"Then the Lord said to Joshua, 'Do not be afraid; do not be discouraged. Take the whole army with you, and go up and attack Ai. For I have delivered into your hands, the king of Ai, his people, his city, and his land.'" Joshua 8:1 (NIV)

1. CHAMPIONS MUST CONFRONT THEIR FEARS.

CHAMPIONS MUST CONFRONT THEIR FEARS. You can only free yourself from fear by facing them. Fears come in many faces. If we aren't careful, we will deal with the fruit of fear and not the root of it. We must always remember that fear is a secondary emotion!

If you have studied emotions, you know that some say there are about eight primary emotions, including anger, shame, disgust, joy, fear, etc. Secondary emotions are emotional reactions. For example, a person may feel ashamed because of becoming anxious or sad. In this case, anxiety would be the primary emotion, while shame would be the secondary emotion.

The beliefs that we get from our experiences often cause secondary emotions. Since our behaviors are born out of our emotions, it makes us ask, "How do we react?" Some people may believe that being fearful is a sign of weakness. Therefore, it can trigger a secondary emotion like anger or anxiety. We can learn to react to our feelings constructively or destructively. We must understand, if we have low esteem, it is centered in fears. Although low self-esteem is characterized by a lack of confidence and feeling badly about oneself, these secondary. People with low self-esteem often feel unlovable, awkward, or incompetent which derives from some type of fear.

We must learn to confront our insecurities, jealousies, or anything that will break our focus on what is essential. Confront whatever you are afraid of every day, and you will win over it. Ralph Waldo Emerson said, "Do the thing you fear, and the death of fear is certain."

Fear prevents you from staying true to yourself. Sadly, potential champions remain unrecognized because of the fear they feel. For example, if you become fearful when you are outside your comfort zone, you might not go to the next level or never achieve your goal. Let's examine several fear factors that could potentially stop you from being a champion.

Here are seven fears preventing potential champions from fulfilling their destiny.

a. Fear of failure

I should have applied for the job as a Director. This was a prized position in my workplace, but I never took that step because I felt I was not qualified, nor would I succeed. I was temporarily put in an acting Director job for about nine months. Though many thought I could do the job, I didn't believe I could do it. I was too afraid I would fail if I was permanently given the job.

Fear kept the Israelite army from fighting Goliath and the Philistine armies. Fear kept someone from confronting Goliath for 40 days. However, fear was not found in David.

b. Fear of being rejected

I never entered Grad School because I imagined my application being rejected. I never applied for jobs because I feared rejection, and I never joined certain groups because I felt I was going to be rejected.

The fear of rejection will stop you from starting. I only imagine that many of Saul's soldiers could have taken on Goliath. However, they were probably hearing that Saul would not allow them. Or someone in the officer's rank may have wanted to step up. However, because of the fear of being rejected by their leader, they never step forward.

Remember the story of the stewards. Three people were given the opportunity to make a return on the owner's investment. Two invested. One didn't: he thought he was going to lose the investment and be in trouble with the owner. Because he thought he would be rejected, he didn't invest. The owner took what he gave him back and called him wicked and kicked him out.

Champions don't see themselves ever being rejected. They moved in faith believing that someone will receive them. Joshua was commanded by God to go forth in battle. He didn't worry about being rejected because God gave him command. You don't have to worry or be afraid about being rejected when you know God has commanded you to go forward.

c. Fear of speaking in public

I never gave big speeches in large audiences because I was afraid of public speaking. Some of my pastor friends have large churches, and I would sneak in and sit in the back because I didn't want them to ask me to speak or say hello to the crowd.

If you are going to be a champion you must speak. No one spoke to Goliath. Goliath insulted them for weeks. He left the comfort of his men and stood out alone taunting the Israelite army. The Bible called Goliath a "champion." He wasn't afraid to speak in public.

David (God's champion) stood in front of everyone and shouted back at Goliath when he shouted at him. God's Champion confronts what is challenging them. They don't feel intimidated. Moses was afraid to speak in public, but God encouraged him.

You must take the Nike slogan Just Do It to heart. If you know what you are talking about, speak boldly. The fact of the matter is, somebody isn't going to like you whether you speak in public or private. God got you. Your voice has power. Use it to the glory of God. It will be alright.

d. Fear of what's happening in the world

I would not travel to certain places because people said terrible things were going on. I was afraid to go to Africa because people told me it was "dangerous" over there. I would not go to lunch with a particular group of people because others said "those aren't good people."

You can't let what others say keep you from moving forward. The army of Israel listened to what Goliath said he was going to do to them and their army. They were afraid and for days they did nothing, because they heard how big Goliath was and how he had this massive set of weaponry.

In Genesis, Moses sent spies into the land to see the areas God would give them. Ten of the twelve spies provided an evil report that they couldn't take the land. Only two said they were able to go in and conquer it. The other ten spies testified they looked like grasshoppers in the eyes of their opponents. They thought that the people in the land would destroy God's people and reported that to Moses and the rest of people. Only two (Joshua and Caleb) believed they could take the land and those were the only two of the original group that went in and enjoyed the land.

You can't focus on what you hear from people, in the news or social media and let those messages override what God is saying. Media houses are witnessing what they see and are willing to walk accordingly. However, believers (champions) walk by faith and not by sight.

. . .

e. Fear of leaving a comfort zone

I was afraid to move to New Orleans because I wasn't comfortable with big cities. My discomfort with big cities came from hearing so much negative talk from those who were fleeing them. I became uncomfortable with going to any town that was larger than my hometown which was about 15,000 people at the time.

You should be ready to move out of your comfortable job to a new position or a new business. You must face your fear: just about everyone I know who is achieving success faces discomfort.

We must "become comfortable with being uncomfortable." But that didn't make sense. The more I watched others achieve their goals, I noticed there were times when they weren't sure if what they were doing was going to work. They were nervous, even frightened that they would be embarrassed or humiliated. However, they pressed through it.

Champions are humans who experience the same challenges as "normal people." They have just decided to let any useful information push them from discomfort to comfort. David was hearing from Goliath that he was going to defeat him. He was hearing criticism from his family. He heard from Saul that he was just a boy and not an experienced fighter. Don't you think that David may have been a little uncomfortable? Remember how uncomfortable Moses was. Remember how Gideon was uncomfortable. However, they pressed forward. You must press your way through. The Apostle Paul says, "I press on toward the goal to win the prize." The victory will be after pressing through uncomfortable situations. Your blessing is on the other side of the pressing.

f. Fear of experiencing the possible outcome

I had the fear of not starting a business because I thought that the government would come and take it all away if I didn't file my taxes or said something wrong in my application process. I had the fear of flying. I had fears that I wouldn't live long because I would be killed by drugs or drug dealers.

This place of fear and apprehension is where most people live who experience high anxiety. Many not only think the worst things possible will happen, they also begin to experience panic attacks from those thoughts.

As a project manager, we had to think of worst-case scenarios and put plans in place just in case they occurred. These exercises kept us calm when things started to go wrong. Why? Because we knew it could occur and already planned on what to do.

When we consider the most severe possible outcome that can reasonably occur in a given situation and put a plan in place, it makes it easier to handle. Now you are just doing the next thing on the checklist. Conceiving worst-case scenarios is a form of strategic planning that prepares you if something happens. Planning reduces stress because now you can focus on solutions that you control. Champions plan and prepare for the worst. David prepared for Goliath. He had a sling and five rocks. The worst that David thought was that he would have five chances to hit Goliath. His worst case did not happen because he hit him the first time and killed him. David planned. Just like when David noticed Saul was getting angry, he planned to play music.

> *"And whenever the harmful spirit from God was upon*
> *Saul, David took the lyre and played it with his hand.*
> *So Saul was refreshed and was well, and the harmful*
> *spirit departed from him." 1 Samuel 16:2 (ESV)*

Saul's men noticed that an evil spirit would come upon Saul and planned for the situation. They didn't just let Saul act crazy but put a plan in place to calm him. Champions plan for the worst case they can imagine and move forward.

g. Fear of the unknown

I had a fear of traveling when I was in Germany because I didn't know what was outside of the walls of the base where I was assigned. I didn't take advantage of traveling to many of the landmarks that are historical because I didn't know what would happen.

Let's look at David's unknowns. He didn't know how to wear armor. He didn't know traditional warfare. He didn't know what the king had to offer. He didn't know how Goliath would fight. Any of these could lead to fears. But champions or winners overcome their fear of the unknown by getting information. Generally, the unknown can be discovered with time.

In my job, I learned the concepts of "known unknowns" and "unknown unknowns." In learning about each of these, it taught me to prepare for them to be there. This brought comfort to those who were fearful to move forward. We didn't let them stop us from getting things done. We just work to find out what could possibly hinder our progress. When you are faced with the "unknowns," work on them. If you know you don't know if a person has money, this is called a "known unknown." Ask the person and you will know. If you don't know if someone is going to show up and shoot up the place, this is an "unknown unknown" (unexpected or unforeseeable conditions). In either case, these fears in our world are called risks. We document what we know, make plans and move forward.

David didn't let the fear of the unknown stop him. He trusted God. You must be like David.

2. CHAMPIONS OVERCOME THEIR WORRIES BY AND THROUGH THE WORD OF GOD

There are giants in our lives we must overcome and thoughts we must deal with. If not, they will cause us to live defeated and unhappy. There are strongholds that will keep us from experiencing a lifetime of joy and peace. Each of these thoughts causes us to be emotionally inept. They will cause many negative emotions, which cause us to walk like a victim instead of a champion.

The scriptures command us not to be afraid, be discouraged or worry. Each of these are displays of fear. We must manage worry and anxiety as champions. Note what God says:

"An anxious heart weighs a man down, but a kind word cheers him up." Proverbs 12:25 (NIV)

An anxious heart is a heart filled with worry. Do you have constant panic attacks? They are associated with your fears. I know they aren't easy to let go and release to God. Let God help you. This is what Isaiah 41 says:

> "I took you from the ends of the earth, from its farthest
> corners I called you I said, 'You are my servant.' I
> have chosen you and have not rejected you. 10 So do
> not fear, for I am with you; do not be dismayed, for I
> am your God. I will strengthen you and help you: I
> will uphold you with my righteous right hand." Isaiah
> 41:9-10. (NIV)

Notice he says, "Do not be dismayed." Do not panic, be troubled, or disturbed. God is with you. Therefore, there is no need to worry. The confidence of a champion is born in trust in God, not in fear. We have boldness in knowing we can achieve anything regardless of the obstacles or problems. We can do all things through Christ Jesus and triumph through Him, who strengthens and empowers us.

We have learned that fear and worry are the Devil's anointing. Fear and worry have no place in the life of Christians. Whatever that comes against us, God will deliver us from it. David said in 1 Samuel 1:37: *"The Lord who rescued me from the claws of the lion and the bear will rescue me from this Philistine."* (NLT)

In other words, David is saying that we shouldn't be afraid of the giant because God will rescue us. If you are going to defeat worry or fear, we must rise from our low places and go up higher. Worry traps people with thoughts of the worst that will happen to them, and it steals their focus from thinking about hope and a good future.

Go to Luke 12:22, when Jesus said to his disciples:

> "22 Therefore I tell you, do not worry about your life,
> what you will eat; or about your body, what you will
> wear. 23 For life is more than food and the body more
> than clothes. 24 Consider the ravens: They do not sow
> or reap, they have no storeroom or barn, yet God feeds
> them. And how much more valuable you are than

*birds! 25 Who of you by worrying can add a single
hour to your life? 26 Since you cannot do this very
little thing, why do you worry about the rest?
27 Consider how the wildflowers grow. They do not
labor or spin. Yet I tell you, not even Solomon in all
his splendor was dressed like one of these. 28 If that is
how God clothes the grass of the field, which is here
today, and tomorrow is thrown into the fire, how
much more will he clothe you — you of little faith!"*
(AMP)

Jesus is teaching about money and possessions. Listen to what he
says about being afraid and worried. Yes, when you walk in fear, you
worry. Worry is nothing but fear and fear is the absence of trust or
assurance or lack of self-confidence.

Well, little faith leaves the door open for fear. I guess little faith is
better than no faith at all. You don't even get out the boat with no
faith, but with little faith, you at least get out.

Champions don't worry because they know that God is their
provider. He provides the strength and necessary food. The below
admonishes us to do the opposite of worry. When it comes to having
food and clothes, we should have confidence God will provide.

*"29 And do not set your heart on what you will eat or
drink; do not worry about it. 30 For the pagan world
runs after all such things, and your Father knows that
you need them. 31 But seek his Kingdom, and these
things will be given to you as well."* (NIV)

3. NEGATIVE THOUGHTS ARE WHAT CAUSE YOU FEAR AND WORRY

If you focus more on the giant than God and listen to what your giant
is saying he will do, you will trust that more than God. If your
thoughts are dominated with negative thoughts, you will put your
trust in what you don't want to happen than what you do want.

*"**32** Do not be afraid, little flock, for your Father has been
pleased to give you the Kingdom." Luke 12:32 (KJV)*

The best way not to worry is to focus on the solution more than
the problem. Notice, God says you are more valuable than a bird and
he takes care of it. Focus on you are valuable and God will take care
of you.

When we seek God's Kingdom first, He promises to provide all of
our needs. Don't worry about where you are going to live because he
promises to give you houses you did not build. Don't worry about
what you are going to eat because he provides. Don't worry about your
flowers blooming, He's got that, too. God promised to take care
of you.

Don't worry or be afraid, for it is God's great joy to give you the
Kingdom. Nothing is missing in heaven nor the Kingdom.

Romans 8:32 says, *"Since he did not spare even his own Son but gave
him up for us all, won't he also give us everything else?"* (NLT)

Did you see that God doesn't spare anything for you? He will give
you "everything else?" Why worry if you know He is going to provide?
By confronting your fears, you will experience freedom, so face your
insecurities, jealousies, or anything that will break your focus on what's
important.

Champions overcome their fears, and as believers, we understand
that fear doesn't come from God. It is from the Devil, therefore, we
should refuse to carry it. We use the Word and Power of God to defeat
worries, and we must trust God over our fears.

Champions overcome concerns, and you are a champion, so
overcome!

As we defeat fear, we move on to excellence. It is hard to achieve
excellence if you don't believe you can't achieve it because you are in
fear. Let move on forward to the next level of being a champion.
Excellence! Let's talk about excellence in Chapter Six.

6

CHAMPIONS EXCEL

*"But since you excel in everything -- in faith, in speech, in
knowledge, in complete earnestness and in the love we
have kindled in you -- see that you also excel in this
grace of giving." 2 Corinthians 8:7 (NIV).*

DID YOU GET IT? Failure is not an option nor is mediocrity. I believe
that David was a man of excellence who took care of business. If you
are going to take on a lion and a bear as your duty, you must believe in
exceling. For some people, when the job gets tough, they get going.
No, no: the saying is, "When the going gets tough, the tough get
going." This realization means you are tough enough to handle it. You
toughen up, and you get better.

We are encouraged to excel in several areas of our lives. You know
what Paul's charge to the church at Corinth was: The previous read
tells us the areas to excel.

In verse 7 listed above, the word "excel" is also translated
"abound." The Greek Word for "abound," according to Strong's
Concordance, is from a root word *perissos*, which means "exceeding
some number or measure or rank or need; over and above, more than
is necessary, superadded; exceeding abundantly, supremely."

God wants you to go above what is required; He wants you to do more than what is necessary. He wants you to excel at EVERYTHING you do. In fact, look at previous verse in New Living Translation:

> *"7 Since you excel in so many ways — in your faith, your*
> *gifted speakers, your knowledge, your enthusiasm, and*
> *your love from us — I want you to excel in this*
> *gracious act of giving." 2 Corinthians 8:7 (NLT).*

How is your giving? Paul here was talking about money and about giving to the work of the ministry. He hit the nail on the head with this church. He didn't mince words. Now this is important that we understand champions or people who succeed are good and exceptional in a number of areas. Many focused on their craft and not the skills that will move them higher. For example, you can be the best carpenter but you don't know how to talk to people. Or you can be the best speaker, but don't know what you are talking about due to your lack of knowledge on a particular topic.

Let's look at some key areas you must master or excel in to be a champion:

1. CHAMPION OF FAITH

I don't know any champion who doesn't have faith. They are often seen as being highly confident that they are going to win. The trust that whatever they are facing can and will be conquered.

The root word for "faith" is "Trust." As you do well in trusting God, you do well in believing that God will make things happen. We are faith-walkers and not just faith-talkers. You are going to need tremendous faith. Your faith must grow because what you had faith for during your last challenge may not be good for the battle you are in now.

Champions understand that with each battle, their faith is challenged. The only way your faith is going to grow is by exercising it or a better way to state it is that "your faith is tested."

> *"3 Be assured that the testing of your faith [through*
> *experience] produces endurance [leading to spiritual*
> *maturity, and inner peace]." James 1:3 (AMP*

James tells us that testing our faith through experience produces endurance which leads to maturity and peace. Your faith is only tested through experience. You don't get faith by only hearing or listening about it: you need to exercise that faith so it can grow.

James also says faith without works is dead (James 2). Again, you need to show you have faith by your actions. Each believer should excel in their faith. Faith isn't stagnant. It is a seed. Seeds produce when planted in the right environment.

David grew and excelled in his faith. He went from killing a lion and a bear to killing Goliath. He increased in courage. He then went from destroying Goliath to killing the Philistine armies. Again, his confidence and trust grew through victory at different levels and in different circumstances.

Remember Gideon. Gideon went from one level of faith to another. He went from fearfully hiding with no courage to tearing down his father's altar to Ba'al and cutting down the Asherah pole to mustering enough courage to amass an army of over 32,000 men (Judges 6-7). His faith level was very low and caused him to hide from the Midianites. However, a word from the angel, "Might Man of Valor," spoke to the champion within him. After speaking with the angel and experiencing the "fleece test," his faith grew. His faith grew because he listened to the Word of the Lord and experienced small victories.

You must listen to someone that is able to stir up the champion within. Your faith will grow as you walk it out. You must receive the instruction from the Lord and move forward. God will be with you every step of the way. Don't worry if it doesn't look like you think it should. Just have faith in God and trust He knows how to bring victory.

Our attitude should be, "I will trust God to be with me no matter what I face."

2. CHAMPION OF SPEECH

You can be the best leader, but if you can't explain what you are doing you will have problems. You might be the best singer, but if you can't tell your story, you will limit yourself.

We should excel in speaking. Now if you have the fear of speaking, you should know that this fear is a trick of the Devil. You need to get out of your own head. You can speak. God has given you the "spirit of public speaking." Victor Chapter 1, Verse 1.

I had to be delivered from the fear of speaking in public. Now I started public speaking as a preteen. We had Christmas and Easter speeches we gave as kids. I always wanted to give long speeches. One reason was because I couldn't really read but I could remember what was said to me. I also taught Sunday School as a teen and young adult, all while afraid of speaking in public. Even as a preacher and leader at work, I suffered from the fear of speaking publicly. As a Senior Manager and Acting Director, I delegated my speaking in large settings to others due to "fear." Even today I hate speaking in large sittings.

Yes, I had to take speaking classes to improve myself. I was a member of Toastmasters and took other public speaking classes to learn how to speak, conduct a meeting, mentor, and coach. I had to learn how to be concise and how to break topics down to be understood. I needed to learn these basic ideas. This is a constant challenge for those of us who are not naturally gifted. Therefore, we must practice, practice, and practice some more.

Paul said, "you excel in so many ways….gifted speaking…" Yes, even the gifted speaker can excel more.

But what if I don't speak well, you may ask. Well, the truth is many of us don't "speak well." However, if you know this and decide to retreat into silence, how are others going to appreciate the value you have? It is like putting a valuable piece of art in the attic. Who can appreciate it there?

Listen what God said to Moses, who didn't speak well: "*But Moses pleaded with the LORD, 'O Lord, I'm not very good with words. I never have been, and I'm not now, even though you have spoken to me. I get tongue-tied, and my words get tangled.' 11 Then the Lord asked Moses,*

'Who makes a person's mouth? Who decides whether people speak or do not speak, hear or do not hear, see or do not see? Is it not I, the Lord? 12 Now go! I will be with you as you speak, and I will instruct you in what to say.'"
Exodus 4:10 (NLT)

What can we learn from Moses to excel?

- He thought he didn't speak well
- He examined his speaking from the past and current situation to plead with God
- His talking to God didn't increase his confidence to speak
- He wanted to cancel out future speaking opportunities based on his present thinking
- He looked at his current condition (stuttering) to keep him from trying

Do we think like this? Oftentimes, people who have the fear of public speaking are judging themselves from some previous bad situation. For example, someone may have put them on the spot and they weren't prepared to speak. Or someone ridiculed the way they spoke and they continue to believe it. Or they might speak slowly and thought it wasn't good enough because they see others who are much more "eloquent."

Thoughts like these will cause us not to excel. If we continue to operate from a point of negative thinking we will not move forward even if God is speaking to us. We listen to God and go. God asked Moses, "Who makes a person's mouth, decides whether people speak, hear, or see?" Then God told him, "Is it not I, the Lord?" That wasn't a question for Moses to ponder. God answered it with his next words, "Now go! I will be with you as you speak"

God has been telling you to go. He made your mouth and eyes and ears and knows your capabilities. When you speak, He is right there with you. You don't have to worry about messing up. Be obedient. Jesus gives us this confidence in Luke: *"11 And when they bring you unto the synagogues, and unto magistrates, and powers, take ye no thought how or what thing ye shall answer, or what ye shall say: 12 For the Holy Ghost shall teach you in the same hour what ye ought to say."* (Luke 12:11-12 (KJV)

Isn't this what God was guaranteeing to Moses when he said I will be with you. Jesus is saying that if you are obedient, God will be with you when you open your mouth. Rely on him. Champions rely on God speaking through them. Champions with the authority of heaven.

3. CHAMPION OF KNOWLEDGE

Our attitude should be, "I am going to prepare the best I can and God will be with me when I speak."

You can be the best speaker but don't know what you are talking about. You can believe you have superior knowledge, but soon come to find out you don't. It is very important that we have knowledge.

We must excel in knowledge. When we have knowledge, it is easier to speak confidently. But we must keep learning, Paul charged to the church again as they have excelled in knowledge.

Champions don't just rely on their faith and ability to speak, they have knowledge. Champions know their opponents. Your opponent may be a person, place,thing, emotion or fear. If you don't know what you are dealing with, you will easily be intimidated by it, underestimate it or make assumptions about it that will cause you to be defeated.

Champions possess knowledge of their strengths and limitations. They know what their enemy can easily exploit and put guards in place to protect vulnerable areas.

They have knowledge and never stop receiving it. They are humble enough to receive instructions from those they like and those they don't. It doesn't matter if your enemy gives you good information or a friend.

Champions know their knowledge starts with God but comes through people as well. Let's look at two scriptures, one from Proverbs, one from Job:

"27 When disaster comes over you like a storm, when trouble strikes you like a whirlwind, when pain and

trouble overwhelm you. 28 Then you will call to Me, but I will not answer. You will look for me, but you will not find me. 29 It is because you <u>rejected knowledge</u> and did not choose to respect the Lord. 30 You did not accept my advice, and rejected my correction." Proverbs 1:27-30 NCV

"3 With my knowledge I will speak comprehensively." Job 36:3 NET

We know that without knowledge, people often fail. But sometimes we can have knowledge and reject it. Either way, you fail. You remember King Saul. In 1 Samuel chapter 15, God sent the prophet Samuel to instruct King Saul to, "Go and attack the Amalekites! Destroy them and all their possessions. Don't have any pity. Kill their men, women, children, and even their babies. Slaughter their cattle, sheep, camels, and donkeys." Saul, however, decided to keep the best sheep and cattle and destroyed everything else. Saul rejected "knowledge." Because he rejected knowledge, God rejected him.

God is the source of knowledge. If we reject Him, where are we going to find knowledge for ourselves? Sometimes, looking for knowledge without God might work but odds are we'll end up with something bad or that doesn't serve us well. Now this isn't to say we don't listen to people. People can be a good source of knowledge, but, if we are not accepting the knowledge God has given us, we will fail.

There was a different situation with Gideon. He did what God commanded him. Though he was afraid of the people, God told him to destroy his father's idols to Ba'al. Gideon sneaked in one night and did it.

Judges 6:25-27 : *"25 That night the Lord said to him, 'Take the bull from your father's herd, as well as a second bull, one that is seven years old. Pull down your father's Ba'al altar and cut down the nearby Asherah pole. 26 Then build an altar for the Lord your God on the top of this stronghold according to the proper pattern. Take the second bull and offer it as a burnt sacrifice on the wood from the Asherah pole that you cut down.' 27 So Gideon took ten of his servants and did just as the Lord had told him.*

He was too afraid of his father's family and the men of the city to do it in broad daylight, so he waited until nighttime. " (NET)

What knowledge of God are you rejecting because of fear? Gideon didn't allow his fear to stop him from obeying God. Samuel explained to Saul that "obedience is better than sacrifice." It was better for Saul to obey God's command to destroy everything (including the best sheep and goats) than Saul thought of keeping the best animal sacrifice for God. It was better for Gideon to destroy what God told him to then to be too afraid of what the people would do to him. Obeying God's word is always better.

The attitude of a champion is, "It is better to obey God in fear than disobey him in faith."

4. CHAMPION OF ENTHUSIASM

This idea entails passion, excitement, fire in the belly, and zeal. You can excel in faith, speech and knowledge, but if you don't have fire in your belly, you may be overtaking or not move high.

It is important as a champion that you have passion about what you are doing. A champion is one that is fighting for a cause. They are passionate about what they are fighting for. This is why it is hard to get them off focus.

I have seen people who are championing a cause who will not take "no" for an answer. The passion for what they are doing often blinds them to defeat. They see negative things happening around them, but their passion for what they believe is able to push them and even cause others to join their cause.

I love what Paul says about the church at Corinth: *"2 for I already know that you are on board and eager to help. I keep boasting to the churches of Macedonia about your passion to give, telling them that the believers of Corinth have been preparing to give for a year. Your enthusiasm is contagious—it has stirred many of them to do likewise."* 2 Corinthians 9:2 (TPT)

Notice that enthusiasm is "contagious." It is good to be around winners. People are drawn to people who are winners. Winners are excited. You must learn that enthusiasm can be stirred up or killed.

I tell my children all the time, "They were created to change the atmosphere." When they are joking, playing sports, singing or worshipping, people are edified. What you do impacts others.

The church at Corinth was so enthused about giving that it caused others to be equally excited. Paul got so excited he used their passion to pass on to the church in Macedonia.

You can't overdo enthusiasm. I know people used to tell me to turn it down when I would walk in the room laughing and joking and having fun. I started to dial it back, but God has since corrected me. I don't need anyone's permission to be passionate about what God has done. Stop letting people take your joy. Stop letting people shut you down because you have a different passion than them. God uniquely made each of us.

In fact, take a look about the "knowledge" you should have on being passionate or enthusiastic about the church:

> "**12** And that's what's happening among you. You are so passionate about embracing the manifestations of the Holy Spirit! Now become even more passionate about the things that strengthen the entire church." 1 Corinthians 14:12 (TPT)

Sometimes, I see there are people who are more passionate about the gifts of the Spirit and their manifestation than they are about what strengthens the church. Paul saw this also in the early church. His point is not to lessen their excitement about the gifts but to emphasize that our passion should be to strengthen one another.

You must excel in your passion. The more you learn who you are and what you are called to do, the more your passion will grow.

The attitude of a champion is, "I bring passion to my party because He has given me victory."

5. CHAMPION OF LOVE

Love God and love people. These two commandments are vital, so be excellent in loving God and loving people.

You can't be a champion for God without loving what you do. You can't be a champion of a cause without love. You can't serve God or people without love.

> *"37 Jesus replied: 'Love the Lord your God with all your heart and with all your soul and with all your mind.' 38 This is the first and greatest commandment. 39 And the second is like it: 'Love your neighbor as yourself.' 40 All the Law and the Prophets hang on these two commandments." Matthews 22:37-40 (NIV)*

Too many people don't know how important love is and how it influences every area of our lives. Love is a verb. It is an action word. We don't just feel love, we "do" love. To tell us to grow or excel in love means that love is not stagnant. We never reach the top of our love ladder. The more you love, the more you receive love.

One of the biggest mistakes we make is to think that we run out of love. Love never ceases. You can never run out of it. Look at something Jesus says about love:

> *"37 Jesus answered him, 'Love the Lord your God with every passion of your heart, with all the energy of your being, and with every thought that is within you.' 38 This is the great and supreme commandment. 39 And the second is like it in importance: 'You must love your friend in the same way you love yourself.' 40 Contained within these commandments to love you will find all the meaning of the Law and the Prophets." Matthew 22:37 (TPT)*

Notice the words "every passion," "all the energy," and "every thought." This leaves nothing out. Passion has to do with emotion. Energy has to do with the physical. Thoughts have to do with knowledge. This means we are fully in as it relates to loving God. We just don't love God with our speech (Lord I love you). You put passion and energy into your loving Him.

Loving God is nothing haphazard. Your focus and purpose is to love him in your daily actions. You look for ways to love him. You excel in loving God in your knowledge. That means you learn daily how to love God.

You also learn to excel in loving others. Again, love is an action word. 1 Corinthians 13 tells us ways to love. Notice, this is telling us how to be in order to love:

> "2 And if I were to have the gift of prophecy with a profound understanding of God's hidden secrets, and if I possessed unending supernatural knowledge, and if I had the greatest gift of faith that could move mountains, but have never learned to love, then I am nothing.

> "3 And if I were to be so generous as to give away everything I owned to feed the poor, and to offer my body to be burned as a martyr, without the pure motive of love, I would gain nothing of value.

> "4 Love is **large and incredibly patient.** Love is **gentle** and **consistently kind to all.** It **refuses to be jealous** when blessing comes to someone else. Love **does not brag about one's achievements nor inflate its own importance.** 5 Love **does not traffic in shame and disrespect,** nor **selfishly seek its own honor.** Love is **not easily irritated or quick to take offense.** 6 Love **joyfully celebrates honesty and finds no delight in what is wrong.** 7 Love is a **safe place of shelter,** for it **never stops believing the best for others.** Love **never takes failure as defeat,** for it **never gives up.** 8 Love never **stops loving.**" 1 Corinthians 13:2-8a (TPT)

I know many have read these verses from other translations or from other references, therefore, let me challenge you to open yourselves to see how to grow in your love by using other translations. It is through others teaching me that I learn how to love myself, how to love others, and, more importantly, how to love God.

I found out that love first has to begin with my understanding of what love is and what it is not. I was often driven by my feelings. I had to learn that feelings were based on my knowledge. I was taught how to feel some things.

For example, people told me I should be angry when certain things are said to me; thus, I became angry when I was disagreed with. Just as we learn to feel anger by what we are taught, we can learn to "feel" love. That is why it is important to ensure we guard what we hear and keep those lessons in mind. Knowledge is powerful.

In the text we learn that love has a lot to do with us changing and responding rather than what others do or say to us. We can love people despite how they treat us if we endeavor to excel in love.

What I do is for the betterment of others. My love doesn't have room to do others wrong. We often say God gave us Ten Commandments. Well Jesus set some of the commands up in the two statements of "loving God" and "loving others." We strive everyday to grow in our love for God and our love for others. We don't look for ways to retreat from God and others. It is commanded that we love people. You must do this. Don't let others cause you to reject God's word because of the way you and they feel about someone.

From the scriptures above, did you notice the action verbs? Did you notice: there are certain areas where love never stops, always goes, never gives up, always believes, consistently is, etc. Go back and see how you can apply love to help you to have victory using these verses.

The attitude of a champion is: My actions say, "I love God and I love people."

6. CHAMPION OF GIVING

For some reason, we can talk about the importance of excelling in faith, speech, knowledge, zeal (enthusiasm), and love. When we start discussing giving, however, everyone wants to pray.

We can talk about our lack of worship. We can talk about not forgiving one another. We can talk about not participating in church activities, but when we start talking about money, we want to pray.

"I want you to excel in giving," is what Paul is writing about. It is clear from both Chapters Eight and Nine, Paul is talking about receiving an offering (collection of money). Paul even uses another church's example to write to another church. He compares their level of giving and enthusiasm. Let's listen to the words and learn how to give of yourself to others and our resources. We are to be the example for others to see. It doesn't matter your age or financial status when it comes to giving.

> "*1 I really do not need to write you about this help for God's people. 2 I know you want to help. I have been bragging about this to the people in Macedonia, telling them that you in Southern Greece have been ready to give since last year. And your desire to give has made most of them ready to give also. 3 But I am sending the brothers to you so that our bragging about you in this will not be empty words. I want you to be ready, as I said you would be. 4 If any of the people from Macedonia come with me and find that you are not ready, we will be ashamed that we were so sure of you. (And you will be ashamed, too!) 5 So I thought I should ask these brothers to go to you before we do. They will finish getting in order the generous gift you promised so it will be ready when we come. And it will be a generous gift — not one that you did not want to give." 2 Corinthians 9:1-5 (NCV)*

Now I see people cherry-picking through this list of faith, speech, knowledge, zeal, love, etc., thinking, "I can only be excellent in one thing." But hold on, please! Can I challenge you to be a champion of all? Yes, you can be a champion in all things! Paul told the church at Philippi, *"13 I can do all things through Christ, because he gives me strength."* Phillipian 4:13 (NCV)

Notice Paul compares not the amount of their giving but their heart for giving. Giving is about the heart. Almost everything we do is influenced by money. Whether it is food, clothes, houses: how much we can have depends on how much we can afford. God supplies our needs, but He ensures we have money to do it or he gifts it to us from someone who paid for it.

Why do we need to excel in giving? Let's get back and see what the Bible tells us from 2 Corinthians 9 (TPT):

- Giving determines future blessing

> *"6 Remember this: The person who plants a little will have a small harvest, but the person who plants a lot will have a big harvest."* (NLT)

This was a hard thing to understand until I thought about the planting and harvest times for farmers. When farmers sow seed, it is a seed and not the crop. The seed looked nothing like a crop. An apple seed doesn't look like an apple nor a plum seed like a plum. Also, the seed produces more than what is sown. If I plant one seed, I get a tree of fruit. Get it? Now I don't know how many plums will be produced by the one seed but God does. Therefore, He tells us to give and trust him for a big harvest.

- Giving freely shows our gratitude

> *"7 Each of you should give as you have decided in your heart to give. You should not be sad when you give, and you should not give because you feel forced to give. God loves the person who gives happily."* (NLT)

Gratitude depicts readiness to show appreciation. Before and after giving, we should have joy. When we decide what we are going to give, we have peace about it. Know this - we determine what we are going to plant. Some farmers choose to plant corn, while others plant greens and others plant wheat. That is why you should not be sad about what you plant or give. You decide. God lets us decide. He doesn't pressure us to the amount nor the what. Isn't that great? If you have this attitude, you will excel because you are deciding.

I love that God doesn't make me give. He tells me to have a purpose in my heart. I never let others guilt me or pressure me into giving because God doesn't. This is freedom!

- How much we give is determined by our abundance

> *"8 And God can give you more blessings than you need.*
> *Then you will always have plenty of everything —*
> *enough to give to every good work. 9 It is written in*
> *the Scriptures: 'He gives freely to the poor. The things*
> *he does are right and will continue forever.'"* (NIV)

Notice that God determines the amount of return on your investment. He promised that He will give me more than what I need and with enough to give to every good work. Now this will be challenging for some to understand. Let me help.

God expects us to give out of the abundance of what we have. I have learned to give out of what I have. I don't borrow to give. Look at this next scripture:

> *"6 I have applied these things to myself and Apollos*
> *because of you, brothers and sisters, so that through*
> *us you may learn 'not to go beyond what is*
> *written,' so that none of you will be puffed up in*
> *favor of the one against the other. 7 For who*
> *concedes you any superiority? What do you have*
> *that you did not receive? And if you received it,*
> *why do you boast as though you did not?"* 1

Corinthians 4:6-7 (New English Translation)
(NET)

Notice that the text lets us know we receive what we have to give. Wait until God gives to you and gives? I often counsel with people who were depressed and feeling guilty because they took their Need Money and made it their Seed Money. When you plant, God determines the season and determines when your harvest will come, not you. Just remember, when the harvest comes, you will have plenty to give and plenty for your needs.

DON'T GO BROKE BY GIVING FROM A PLACE OF EMOTION! Too many people are broke because they are not giving from sound Biblical teaching on finances. They give based on a "quote" or a "phase" that incite a hope for the future blessing without having a sound strategy to ensure success.

- If you are going to live the abundant life, you must renew your mind and think differently. This requires patients and discipline. You must read books and listen to experts who have been successful. I have learned that people with little can tell me how to be broke and have no expertise on how to live in abundance. Find a "Abraham: to consult if you want the blessings of "Abraham." God determines and gives the seeds to sow what you need to grow.

  "10 God is the One who gives seed to the farmer and bread for food. He will give you all the seed you need and make it grow so there will be a great harvest from your goodness." (NCV)

Wow. God gives us not only what we are going to plant, He tells us to decide what to give. But He gives us the "what" to give. He makes it easy to see what to give. I can't give what He hasn't given me to give. You can't give what He hasn't given you to give.

What He gives you to sow, He expects you to eat from (food to the sower). God expects us to enjoy the harvest or the fruit of our labor. If you aren't receiving a harvest, maybe you are planting something God didn't give you to sow or sowing in a field that is not suited for your seed to produce.

- God determines we will be rich in every way

> *"11 He will make you rich in every way so that you can always give freely. And your giving through us will cause many to give thanks to God. 12 This service you do not only helps the needs of God's people, it also brings many more thanks to God."* (ESV)

This is an area believers must learn to excel in. God said "He will make you rich." Now you have to believe that. There are godly principles rich people live by. You don't just "wish" to be rich, you expect to be if you follow God's principle.

When it comes to being rich or wealthy, God doesn't have a problem with you being so. He set before us blessings and curses. He set before you the ability to earn wealth.

> *17 You may say to yourself, "My power and the strength of my hands have produced this wealth for me." 18 But remember the Lord your God, for it is he who gives you the ability to produce wealth, and so confirms his covenant, which he swore to your ancestors, as it is today." Deuteronomy 8:17-18 (NIV)*

> *"The blessing of the LORD, it maketh rich, and he addeth no sorrow with it." Proverbs 10:22 (KJV)*

> *The blessing of the LORD brings [true] riches, And He adds no sorrow to it [for it comes as a blessing from God]. Proverbs 10:22 (AMP)*

As a champion of the Lord, expect wealth and riches. Remember, you can't just take a few scriptures and quote them without finding the principle that will lead to manifestation. For example, if you want riches, there is work associated with it. We must understand that God gives us the ability to get wealth. The ability doesn't come from "me," it comes from God because His covenant with us.

The English word *power* in Hebrew is *koach* - and literally translates to mean divine power, divine ability, substance, wealth or divine strength to lay hold of something that is beyond our strength to lay hold of. God has given each of us divine empowerment to make a living and create wealth. We should expect an increase from our work to be realized in material gain.

After we prosper, we give. God freely gives to us. You don't have to beg. The blessings of God comes from obedience and/or grace. God isn't using riches or blessing to negotiate favor.

Notice God "make you rich in every way." You want to be rich? Let God do it. There is no sin in being rich. There are rich people who love the Lord. There are rich people who live for God. Why can't you be one of them, too? Have purpose in your heart to be rich and let God do it.

God provides what we need. When God commissions you for the work of the ministry, He will provide.

> *"5 Jesus sent out these twelve, instructing them as follows:*
> *'Do not go on a road that leads to Gentile regions and*
> *do not enter any Samaritan town. 6 Go instead to the*
> *lost sheep of the house of Israel. 7 As you go, preach*
> *this message: The kingdom of heaven is near! 8 Heal*
> *the sick, raise the dead, cleanse lepers, cast out demons.*
> *Freely you received, freely give.'" Matthew*
> *10:5-8* (NET)

When Jesus sent His disciples out, they were given what they needed to succeed. God has given us everything we need for life and godliness (2 Peter 1:3). We excel in the fact that God provides and we, in turn, give from His supply.

- Giving is proof our faith

> *"13 It is a proof of your faith. Many people will praise*
> *God because you obey the Good News of Christ—the*
> *gospel you say you believe—and because you freely*
> *share with them and with all others."* (ESV)

Now that we know that God gives us what to sow and when to sow, we give. When we give, it proves our faith. James said our faith is proven by our acts of services. When we give to others, we demonstrate obedience to God. Don't ever think your giving is in vain. Do not question the amount you give. Give according to what you have and your faith and knowledge.

When it comes to giving, many don't excel in giving because of the fear they hold of not having enough or they don't give because they lack the knowledge they need to understand God's perspective. Maybe you don't give because you truly haven't understood why God commands us to give. If you aren't giving, don't just pray about: be obedient about it.

If you are looking for the best time to give based on your circumstances, you many never give. Many observe what is going on around them and that will determine their giving or if they are going to give or their level of giving. This approach may not be the best thing to do. Notice what the Bible tells us in Ecclesiastes 11:4:

> *"4 Farmers who wait for perfect weather never plant. If*
> *they watch every cloud, they never harvest."* (NLT)

A modern translation says:

> *"Those who wait for perfect weather will never plant seeds;*
> *those who look at every cloud will never harvest*
> *crops." Ecc 11:4* (NCV)

Simply put, if you are looking at what is coming in your paycheck or what is in your bank account only, you will probably not give anything or to the level God expects. Giving is about obedience to God and trusting him to do his part for you.

If you focus on every cloudy day, you will not harvest. Do you know there are people who do not gather because they are afraid of what may happen? This is what the second part of this scripture is describing. I have been like that. I would not receive a blessing from someone because I thought strings were attached. I was looking at "the clouds." Don't miss your blessing thinking receiving will hurt you. Be wise in your giving and in your receiving.

The attitude of a champion who is a giver is, "If God tells you to give, He is saying, 'I will provide the seed and send the harvest.'" The attitude of a champion harvester is "God is providing, it's harvest time." As long as we are here on earth, God will give us the opportunity to plant and harvest.

> "While the earth remains, seedtime and harvest, cold and heat, summer and winter, day and night, shall not cease." Genesis 8:22 (ESV)

Remember, we give from our place of knowledge. Too many of us are using faith alone, which leads to being trapped in disappointments. Use the entire counsel of God's word when it comes to giving and receiving. You must excel in giving and receiving as you excel in the other areas discussed.

If you are going to absorb the champion's mentality, you must first become a champion for excellence, ensuring a 100 percent commitment to whatever you do.

Don't give room for mediocrity in your life. Now moving on, are you willing to pay the price? There is a cost to develop yourself to be all God has called you to be. There is a cost to being excellent. The next chapter describes how champions are always willing to pay the price.

7

CHAMPIONS ARE WILLING TO PAY THE PRICE

EVERYTHING COMES WITH A COST. Experience teaches us that nothing comes free. If a store offers something for free, it is tied to some cost. If it is not money, it is time. If it is not time, it will cost me money. If the item you buy is discounted, the one you need that goes with it as at the regular price or the item is marked up.

I love getting "free trips." With some free trips, I must sit through a presentation on a Timeshare or attend the trip with someone who becomes annoying. There is some cost to "free."

Although we recognize that Salvation is Free, we know that there is a cost for it. Jesus laid down his life so that you and I can freely receive what God has to offer. In order to receive that blessing, it will cost in faith in what Father God and his son, Jesus, have done.

Champions all know that if they are going to succeed, it is going to challenge them to push themselves beyond their competitor. For example, was Michael Jordan born to be the best basketball player in the world? Hardly. He was removed from his high school basketball team during his sophomore year. The other players did something better in the eyes of the coach than Michael. However, he did something that made him become superior and later led him to become the GOAT (Greatest of All Time) in his sport. He decided to outwork his competitors. I can imagine he had to give up hanging with his friends or going on dates in exchange for spending long days and nights on the court. To develop, it cost him.

Was David born to be the only one to kill Goliath? Was he the only one presented with this opportunity? Hardly. The scripture tells us that there were many opportunities for others to step up and take the challenge.

You see, for days, Goliath taunted God's people. Then one day a little shepherd boy was sent by his father to check on his brothers and heard someone defying God's army. We must understand that this giant Goliath was key to David's next assignment. David's goal wasn't just to kill Goliath to make a name for himself. Goliath was between David and his purpose. The cost of meeting the king and receiving the benefit of Saul's kingdom was David standing up to Goliath and the Philistines.

"20 Early in the morning, David left the flock in the care of a shepherd, loaded up and set out, as Jesse had directed. He reached the camp as the army was going out to its battle positions, shouting the war cry. 21 Israel and the Philistines were drawing up their lines facing each other. 22 David left his things with the keeper of supplies, ran to the battle lines, and asked his brothers how they were. 23 As he was talking with them, Goliath, the Philistine champion from Gath, stepped out from his lines and shouted his usual defiance, and David heard it. 24 Whenever the Israelites saw the man, they all fled from him in great fear. 25 Now the Israelites had been saying, 'Do you see how this man keeps coming out? He comes out to defy Israel. The king will give great wealth to the man who kills him. He will also give him his daughter in marriage and will exempt his family from taxes in Israel.' 26 David asked the men standing near him, 'What will be done for the man who kills this Philistine and

*removes this disgrace from Israel? Who is this
uncircumcised Philistine that he should defy the
armies of the living God?'* **27** *They repeated what
they had been saying and told him, 'This is what
will be done for the man who kills him.'" 1 Sam
17:20-27 (NLT)*

David's first reason for fighting Goliath was "God" and his second
reason for fighting was the benefits the king was offering. What price
are you willing to pay to achieve your goal? Do you know what it takes
to become a champion?

There are costs you must be willing to pay to prepare you to be
victorious. As we look at this story, we can discover the cost of his
anointing. Although it wasn't obvious to David that the journey he
was sent on by his father will launch him into his purpose, we can
learn from his journey.

Let's look at this story illustrating obeying a simple routine
instruction:

*"17 Jesse said to his son David, "Take this half bushel of
cooked grain and ten loaves of bread to your brothers
in the camp. 18 Also take ten pieces of cheese to the
commander and to your brothers. See how your
brothers are and bring back some proof to show me
that they are all right. 19 Your brothers are with Saul
and the army in the Valley of Elah, fighting against
the Philistines." 1 Samuel 17:17-19 New Century
Version (NCV)*

1. CHAMPION KNOWS THE IMPORTANCE OF OBEYING SIMPLE ROUTINE INSTRUCTIONS

Jesse and David didn't know that this trip was going to be a defining
moment. David's father was like any normal father who is concerned
about his children. He was sending them a food box much like parents
today sending something to their college student. David was just

supposed to take the food and bring a report back on the status of his siblings.

Now this wasn't David's first trip. In a previous verse, it said he went back and forth between Saul and taking care of his father's sheep. As far as the family knew, David wasn't ready for war, just taking care of sheep and bringing status reports.

You don't know when God will call you to your coming out assignment. God has developed you enough to take your giant. So be careful of neglecting "small and/or routine" assignments. They can lead you to your next big opportunity. Be faithful in the little things.

During the 46th Presidential Inauguration ceremony of President Joseph R. Biden and Vice President Kamala D. Harris, there were so many new faces of highly talented people performing. To get to the big stage, they were in the right place to be discovered just doing what they do in some obscure location across the country. That can be you, and being chosen comes at a cost. Similar to these new stars who were just "doing their thing" to the best of their ability, you need to always do your best knowing that God is preparing you for your coming out party. Destiny is calling you. Be prepared. Champions know the importance of getting an early start.

> **"20** Early in the morning, David left the flock in the care
> of a shepherd, loaded up and set out, as Jesse had
> directed." 1 Sam 17:20 (NIV)

Champions are up early working out and getting fit. They run and exercise, conditioning themselves for the next opponent. They are up in the morning when others are sleeping. They prepare mentally and physically. Champions improve their skills and study their opponents. They become knowledgeable to the point of knowing the little things that will give them an advantage.

We don't just get up early, we get up with a purpose. David got up early. Notice that David got up early, left the flock he usually cared for and prepared for the journey.

First, we must learn to be early. The discipline to getting started early is key for champions. Starting before everyone and spending time praying and planning your journey is a must. Our preparation starts with spending time with God early in the morning.

2. CHAMPIONS KNOWS THE IMPORTANCE OF LEAVING OLD ASSIGNMENTS

> *"David left the flock in the care of a shepherd." 1 Sam 17:20 (NIV)*

Next, David left his old assignment, the flock his once cared for. On your way to the next purpose, you must completely let go of the current assignment. We must understand that our next assignment is a journey away. You can't keep your hands on your current responsibility and go after your next. David had to leave the flock. Certainly he was dedicated to it. He killed a lion and bear to save them. He was passionate in his service as a shepherd. But he had to leave it.

You must release old assignments early. Too often we are thinking too long about what God is separating us from. Our next assignment is going to take all our energies. Decide early to leave things behind, both physically and emotionally.

Notice David just didn't leave the sheep alone. He ensured that he left them in the care of another.

3. CHAMPIONS KNOW THE IMPORTANCE OF LEAVING THEIR PREVIOUS ASSIGNMENT IS GOOD HANDS

> *"David left the flock in the care of a shepherd." 1 Sam 17:20 (NIV)*

Something I've learned is you aren't going to care about your next assignment if you don't care about the one you have.

The cost of leaving the sheep unattended would have shown David's character. Each time you get ready for your next assignment, you should ensure that the current assignment is taken care of. Too often as a Senior Manager and Pastor, I've seen people who want to be promoted just drop their current responsibilities and go after something else. This gave them a bad reputation of not completing assignments or of being an opportunist.

Managers didn't want to hire them because they didn't know if they were going to do the same thing while working for them. Remember, your character goes with you. If you chase one assignment and neglect the one you have, you will not prosper.

David took the time to ensure that the sheep he was responsible for were cared for. It took time for him to do that, but he accounted for it by getting up early and preparing. Which leads to our next cost of being a champion.

4. CHAMPIONS KNOW THE IMPORTANCE OF PREPARING FOR THE NEXT ASSIGNMENT

"David left the flock in the care of a shepherd, loaded up and set out, as Jesse had directed." 1 Sam 17:20 (NIV)

Notice: David loaded up and departed for this next assignment per his father's instruction. When you and I are told that we are going to our next assignment, we must prepare for it. I have learned the importance of preparing for the next journey.

The five "Ps" are my philosophy for being prepared: Proper Preparation Prevents Poor Performance. When David loaded up, he probably knew what was needed for the journey. He probably had food, clothing and the other supplies necessary to ensure they sustained him and others for the trip.

You must "load up." You must prepare yourself for the next assignment God has for you. Don't you know that sometimes your next breakthrough and big shift in God can come from your obedience to and preparation of a little task, little things like bringing food to and checking on your brother.

Don't make light of small assignments and think they are not important. David was thinking he was going out just to check on his brothers. He was only obeying his father's instructions. Yet he didn't take that assignment lightly. He got up early and prepared for the journey.

You must prepare not only for the current assignment, but also for the next one. We know that David prepared to fight Goliath. The Bible said when he was getting ready for his fight, the king wanted David to wear his armor, but it didn't fit.

> *"Saul said to David, 'Go, and may the Lord be with you.'*
> *38 Saul put his own clothes on David. He put a*
> *bronze helmet on his head and dressed him in armor.*
> *39 David put on Saul's sword and tried to walk*
> *around, but he was not used to all the armor Saul*
> *had put on him.*

> *"He said to Saul, "I can't go in this, because I'm not used*
> *to it." Then David took it all off. 40 He took his stick*
> *in his hand and chose five smooth stones from a*
> *stream. He put them in his shepherd's bag and*
> *grabbed his sling. Then he went to meet the*
> *Philistine." 1 Samuel 17:37-39 (NCV)*

David prepared for Goliath by using things he was familiar with. We must learn to use what the Lord has given us for the battles He is calling us to have. Champions use their gifts to win. If your gift is speaking or typing or leading, etc., God is going to use it to launch you into your purpose. You have more in your bag than a sling; you have a stick and rocks. Use them. They are more than enough in God's hand.

For example, I learned how to coordinate small projects well. When I was asked to lead larger ones, it was easy to adapt because I learned the basics of project management. I perfected that when no one was looking. I would be at my desk at night learning the concepts long before I was given a project that required all the concepts to be used. When I got the big job, I was ready because I knew ahead of time what it took to be successful. I was told I should train for the job I want, not the one I have.

This is the principle God gives us in Epheshian chapter 2: *"10 For we are God's handiwork, created in Christ Jesus to do good works, which God prepared in advance for us to do."* Ephesians 2:10 (NIV)

God had predestined David to meet Goliath. He gave David the wisdom to select the weaponry he needed for the battle. He gave him the confidence he needed to speak boldly to Goliath and confidently to Saul, yet David remained humble before God.

David prepared for the journey and once he faced Goliath, he prepared for him. Each assignment requires different preparation. Preparing to fight a lion and bear is different from preparing to fight a Goliath.

You must be willing to change your preparation approach and strategy. I remember when Muhammid Ali was preparing to fight George Foreman in Africa in a fight called the "Rumble in the Jungle." Ali created a strategy called the "The rope-a-dope." It was a boxing technique that he had not used until he studied Foreman's fighting habits. He laid on the ropes most of the fight and let Forman punch himself out. Ali won because he dared to try something different.

God will give you a different strategy as he gave for David and Ali to take out your giants. Don't be afraid of doing something different for the sake of victory.

As a champion, just know that, like David, your journey may lead you to something much bigger than what you started out to achieve. Embrace it. God's got you.

As we look at what it takes to be a champion, we must understand the people are often just ordinary people doing normal tasks. It isn't until God puts an extraordinary situation in front of them, that makes it seems like they are exceptional. You are "exceptional" waiting for an extraordinary challenge to propel you into destiny.

5. CHAMPIONS KNOW THE IMPORTANCE OF BEING A STUDENT

"15 Study and do your best to present yourself to God approved, a workman [tested by trial] who has no reason to be ashamed, accurately handling and skillfully teaching the word of truth." 2 Timothy 2:15 (AMP)

There is nothing more interesting than to get into the mind of a true champion. No matter if that champion is a star quarterback or a star basketball or a tennis player, you know they are students of the game. They study to improve their skills and to know their opponents. Studying is not just reading. It means taking seriously what you are reading and then looking for more within it. You take notes of what you've read, heard, and learned and apply it to your life.

Notice this scripture says "study and do your best." You can't defeat an enemy if you don't know what you are dealing with. You can't defeat an enemy if you don't know what it will take to defeat them. You must study their strengths and weaknesses.

In sports, we learn the importance of knowing your opponents strengths and weaknesses. The coach would spend a lot of time reviewing tapes of the other teams. They want to know the other team's defensive and offensive strengths and weaknesses. They would also have us review the tapes and then have us run the opposing team's plays so that our team would know how to respond. We also have to study individual players so that we could effectively guard and/or block them.

As a champion of the Lord, we take scriptures to defeat our enemy. This is why it is important to study as unto the Lord. The Lord will have you to study the right scripture at the right time so you will be prepared when any day of evil comes.

Champions ensure the information they are receiving about themselves and their opponent is the best and most accurate; their victory depends on it. They take time to verify before moving on the information.

We study because we know we will be tested or challenged. As students, we make certain we are ready for the test. We don't get mad when the test comes because we have prepared for it. We look forward to every trial and test because we know we can't get the crown until we have defeated the opponent.

To develop the warrior that is in you and experience success, you must be a student. Continue to learn ways to win. Continue developing and changing your strategies so that you are ready for all kinds of tests.

6. CHAMPIONS ARE GOOD AT WHAT THEY DO

"Do you see someone skilled in their work? They will serve before kings; they will not serve before officials of low rank." Proverbs 22:29 (NIV)

If you want to be good or the best at anything, you must commit time to it. When I played sports, some of the guys would be on the court for eight hours a day. Now, I wanted to be good, but not eight hours a day good. But I learned that they were much better than me. This was because they were willing to put the time in developing and improving their skills.

The scripture we read in 2 Timothy 3:15 (AMP) tells us to be "*a workman [tested by trial] who has no reason to be ashamed.*" Putting the time in gives you the opportunity for your skills to be tested. The more you test or practice, the better chance for success.

Once your skills are tested and perfected you will find yourself in the presence of greatness. Your skills will make room for you in the presence of kings, says the Bible. The purpose is to improve your skills.

7. CHAMPIONS DO WHAT IS NECESSARY - DENYING ONESELF

Champions don't do what they want. They do what is required. They have to deny themselves in order to stay focused on their goals. Sure, they want to go out and have fun or eat any and everything or hangout with the old crowd. However, they realize if they are going to reach their desired goals, they must ignore or reject things that are adding value.

Denying who we are to become like Him is the ultimate sacrifice because to be the real champion in any endeavor means releasing one's desires, thoughts and time to become who they want to be. Jesus made this plan when explaining what it would take to follow him in Mark 8:34-38.

When He had called the people to Himself, with His disciples also, He said to them: *"34 Whoever desires to come after Me, let him deny himself, and take up his cross, and follow Me. 35 For whoever desires to save his life will lose it, but whoever loses his life for my sake, and the gospels will save it. 36 For what will it profit a man if he gains the whole world and loses his own soul? 37 Or what will a man give in exchange for his soul? 38 For whoever is ashamed of Me and My words in this adulterous and sinful generation, of him, the Son of Man also will be ashamed when He comes in the glory of His Father with the holy angels."* (WEB)

To become a champion for the Lord, you cannot do whatever you feel like doing. You can't follow every urge that comes to your mind. Some measure of control is needed for you to become a champion. This realization is why we are urged in the Bible to guard our hearts with all diligence because out of it are the issues of life (Proverbs 4:23).

What does denying ourselves look like? Why is it necessary to deny yourself?

First, notice the phase "deny yourself." Yes, this has to do with you taking control of what can control you. The Dictionary of Bible Themes defines self-denial as "the willingness to deny oneself possessions or status, in order to grow in holiness and commitment to God."

Denying yourself includes overcoming the fleshly demands of the body, also known as the carnal self or the natural man, and bringing them into submission to God's Word so that you don't give into sin. It also means, denying yourself of pleasures that go against or hinders you from reaching your goal(s).

Self-denial for the Christian means renouncing oneself as the center of existence (which goes against the natural inclination of the human will) and recognizing Jesus Christ as one's new and true center. It means acknowledging that the old self is dead and the new life is now hidden with Christ in God (Colossians 3:3–5).

Champions for the Lord continually put God as the center. They beat down thoughts that will lift them in pride or arrogance.

While guarding your life, become intentional with bold confessions because, as a champion, you are no different from your words. In the next chapter, we will analyze the concept of making bold confessions. The correct confessions keep us focused on what we need to do as it relates to denying oneself.

8

CHAMPIONS HAVE BOLD CONFESSIONS

"I can do all things through Christ who strengthens me."
Phillipians 4:13 (WEB)

THAT'S BOLD. It is awesome to have an attitude that nothing can stop your success because you know God on your side. You don't have to worry about becoming weak because Christ is constantly strengthening you is embodied in this text. Speak it boldly daily.

Successful people must be bold and courageous in their approach to anything: the signs of weakness in a fight encourages your opponent and gives strength to their cause. It was evident that the Israelite army was discouraged. David spoke to this before going out to battle:

> *"32 'Don't worry about this Philistine,' David told*
> *Saul. 'I'll go fight him!' 33 'Don't be ridiculous!' Saul*
> *replied. 'There's no way you can fight this Philistine*
> *and possibly win! You're only a boy, and he's been a*
> *man of war since his youth.' 34 But David persisted.*
> *'I have been taking care of my father's sheep and*
> *goats,' he said. 'When a lion or a bear comes to steal a*
> *lamb from the flock, 35 I go after it with a club and*

rescue the lamb from its mouth. If the animal turns on me, I catch it by the jaw and club it to death. 36 I have done this to both lions and bears, and I'll do it to this pagan Philistine, too, for he has defied the living God's armies! 37 The Lord who rescued me from the claws of the lion and the bear will save me from this Philistine!' Saul finally consented. 'Alright, go ahead,' he said. 'And may the Lord be with you!'"1 Samuel 17:32-37 (NLT)

What boldness. David would not allow anyone to convince him that this fight wasn't his. Notice the confidence he projects. Notice the boldness in speaking to the king, a man of war. Notice the confidence he spoke about of his God's ability to rescue him.

If you are going to be successful, you must find strength in your own voice to speak boldly. You must know who you are and what you are capable of doing and not let anyone talk you out of your victory.

There are some key things to note here:

1. CHAMPIONS SPEAK FAITH

"32 'Don't worry about this Philistine,' David told Saul. 'I'll go fight him!'" (NLT)

Don't be afraid of your enemies; be prepared to fight. David was worried about the giant. You will have a "giant" situation in your life. You must speak from the point of faith. Faith and worry can't occupy the same space.

After hearing what the king would reward the person for killing Goliath, David said "I will fight him." More than that, David spoke confidently about His God. Through this concourse David kept God at the center. He was upset that Goliath was taunting God's army.

When you know your God in the face of trouble, your faith should speak louder than your fears. When you know God is with you, your faith should drive out all fears. Our faith is grounded in knowing

God's ability to rescue us. We are able to speak boldly because our confidence is in God, not in ourselves.

2. CHAMPIONS ENCOURAGE THEMSELVES

A believer must speak boldly and must stop talking negatively. Saul and the others were only talking about what was going on with the Philistines. David, however, only spoke about what his God did, and he encouraged Saul when he sensed discouragement in the ranks.

David encouraged Saul when he spoke of past victories, and he used his experiences with God to support himself and his argument. He wasn't getting any encouragement from those around him.

Champions are able to convince others of what they can do with their God on their side. When others are afraid, you can look back at times when you were in a bind and remember how you got out. As David reminded Saul of the bear and lion and the victories he had, you must look back at times when you thought you were not going to make it and how you made it. Remember to speak victory to your future by remembering the victories of your past. You should always be able to silence the noise of worry when your confidence is in God. When everyone else is speaking of fear and defeat, you speak faith and victory. You are created to change those who are doubting by sharing your testimony of what God has done for you.

3. CHAMPIONS USE TESTIMONIES OF VICTORY TO ENCOURAGE OTHERS

Notice when David gave Saul his testimony: it encouraged Saul to let him go after Goliath. You need to think back at how you overcame challenges. You need to say, "God brought us out before, and He will do it again. He healed me once, He will do it again, and since He provided the last time, He will do it again." What are your confessions of faith? Take action today, and speak God's Word! Are you confessing victory or defeat?

Remember the story of Moses and the Egyptians army? God used his mighty hands to get Pharoah to let his people go and the children of Israel still didn't fully trust God to protect them. Even though he showed powerful miracles of turning water to blood, releasing frogs, pestilence, wild animals, hail, boils on flesh, first born dying, etc., they still didn't trust him. Even though God led them by using a cloud to provide shade for them in the day and a pillar of fire to warm them at night, they still didn't fully trust him. The Israelites didn't use the victories they experienced with God to encourage them along the way.

Even after the Egyptian army was drowned in the sea, the people still rebelled against God. They complained to God who fed them with Manna and didn't let their shoes or clothes wearout.

Moses gave hope, however:

> *"1 Then Moses and the Israelites sang this song to the Lord: 'I will sing to the Lord, for he has triumphed gloriously; horse and rider he has thrown into the sea. 2 The Lord is my strength and my might, and he has become my salvation; this is my God, and I will praise him, my father's God, and I will exalt him. 3 The Lord is a warrior; the Lord is his name. 4 "Pharaoh's chariots and his army he cast into the sea."* Exodus 15:1-4 (NLT)

Now look at his testimony. He used this to remind himself of the faithfulness of God. He, like David, said something about His God - He is my strength, might, salvation, God, I will praise him. You have to learn how to encourage yourself in the Lord.

When you know that God has given you victory in the past, it gives you confidence that He has your future. Trust him. The prophet Jeremiah says this about God:

> *"For I know the thoughts that I think toward you, saith the Lord, thoughts of peace, and not of evil, to give you an expected end." Jeremiah 29:11 (KJV):*

God has an expected end, and it is of peace and not evil. "Not of evil" means "good."

In the New Century Version (NCV) translation, it says: *"I say this because I know what I am planning for you," says the Lord. "I have good plans for you, not plans to hurt you. I will give you hope and a good future."*

Another example we can see is when Moses sent the spies into the land that God promised them. Notice in Numbers Chapter 13 how those who trust God talked, opposed to those who trusted only in themselves.

> *"17 When Moses sent them to explore Canaan, he said, "Go up through the Negev and on into the hill country. 18 See what the land is like and whether the people who live there are strong or weak, few or many. 19 What kind of land do they live in? Is it good or bad? What kind of towns do they live in? Are they unwalled or fortified? 20 How is the soil? Is it fertile or poor? Are there trees in it or not? Do your best to bring back some of the fruit of the land." (It was the season for the first ripe grapes.) 21 So they went up and explored the land*

> *"30 Then Caleb silenced the people before Moses and said, "We should go up and take possession of the land, for we can certainly do it." 31 But the men who had gone up with him said, "We can't attack those people; they are stronger than we are." 32 And they spread among the Israelites a bad report about the land they had explored. They said, "The land we explored devours those living in it. All the people we saw there are of great size. 33 We saw the Nephilim there (the descendants of Anak come from the Nephilim). We seemed like grasshoppers in our own eyes, and we looked the same to them."* (NIV)

Now this is remarkable. God told them He was giving them the land. They were only to investigate the land. They were to assess their skills against anyone else that might be there. Notice they were never told to say, *"We can't attack those people; they are stronger than we are."* They were just supposed to give an assessment of the fruitfulness of the land and the condition of the people. They weren't supposed to determine if the people could defeat them or not. God had already told them He would provide victory.

When you listen to the wrong voices, it will bring fear or cause you to see things differently than God. God has great plans for you. You must confess this every day and build up yourself as a champion mentally and spiritually, as Caleb and Joshua did. The more you say the right words, the more empowered you become, such that your bold words align with your beliefs for success.

Even if everyone around you speaks negatively, remember David, Caleb and Joshua, who amid so much negativity stood up for what they believed, and that was how they got the victory. Positivity also works with optimism. See the good in everything, and you will only have empowering experiences that are common to champions.

In addition to saying the right words and making your bold confessions, you also have to stay committed to your projects and tasks because champions are finishers. We will unearth more about finishing what you start as a champion in the next chapter.

9

CHAMPIONS ARE INVESTED

"And let us not grow weary of doing good, for in due season we will reap, if we do not give up." Galatians 6:9 (ESV)

IN ORDER TO BE A CHAMPION, you must be invested. Another way of saying this is, "You must be committed." Paul J. Meyer states, "Productivity is never an accident. It is always the result of a commitment to excellence, intelligent planning, and focused effort."

There was a story I heard many years ago. It was about three animals on a farm having a conversation: a chicken, pig, and cow. They were talking about breakfast on the farm. During the conversation two of the animals were so excited by how they could contribute. The chicken was excited about how many eggs she could provide. The cow went on and on about the glasses of milk she could provide. However, the pig wasn't so excited. You see the chicken and cow were involved where the pig had to commit his life if bacon was to be served.

How committed are you to winning? How much of you are you willing to invest in your success? How much time or money or even yourself are you willing to give to be at the top?

How much you are willing to invest in your success will determine how many victories you'll have. If you are going to be the best, there are things you must sacrifice. If you are going to be the best, there are some things that are not optional, things you must do.

1. HOW DO YOU INVEST IN YOURSELF?

There are many ways to invest in yourself such as reading books about your business or craft, taking classes or specialized training to improve your skills or listening to podcasts or webinars to enhance your knowledge. We can also invest in ourselves by joining interest groups that will provide new and innovative ways to provide our services.

As we have learned, the Bible tells us to be the best even for God. We do this by studying his word:

> *"15 Do your best to present yourself to God as one*
> *approved, a worker who has no need to be ashamed,*
> *rightly handling the word of truth." 2 Tim*
> *2:15 (ESV)*

Our first charge is to invest in ourselves for God's approval. We study to be the best for Him. *"Surely, no matter what you are doing (speaking, writing, or working)"* (Col 3:17 [Voice Bible]), we do these things as representatives of God. We do our best for him. We invest in ourselves so we don't put him to shame or humiliate ourselves.

2. WHY IS IT IMPORTANT TO INVEST IN YOURSELF?

Investing in yourself will yield great personal benefits. No matter if you invest in your personal life or business, you will get both immediate and long term benefits.

The investment of time, work and money you invest into yourself will directly impact the quality of life you will experience. Many people try to take short cuts. By the time you take all the shortcuts, you will have discovered that to get quality results, it takes focus. You can spend your time or money trying to get ahead. If that time and money is not spent in the correct areas of your life, however, your investment will be wasted. Investing takes time to result in a return. When you invest in yourself, after time it will give you great benefits, many of which you did not think of when you started out.

3. WHAT DOES INVEST IN ME MEAN?

Many of us spend more time investing in others than we do investing in ourselves. It is ok to invest in your kids and think you are investing in you. It is ok to spend a lot of time on your job to produce for them and think it is investing in you. Neither of these may involve an immediate or future investment in you.

Investing in you means that where you spend your time or resources will give "you" benefit. This may sound selfish, but it is not. For example, is it selfish to ask your director for a raise after you have proven yourself to be invaluable to the organization? Is it selfish to ask your kids to take care of your vehicle you need to get back and forth to work? The answer is no.

Therefore, *investing in me* means using money or other resources to improve oneself, one's circumstances, or something else of importance, with the hope and purpose that doing so will bring future benefits.

If you don't invest in upgrading your skills or knowledge, you will become less valuable in your workplace and not in a position for immediate or future benefits.

Now what does the Bible say about investing in you? As we serve others in ministry, at home, or in the workplace, ensuring our skills are current and our bodies are fresh is often neglected. We "know" that we should take better care of ourselves, but there are a number of reasons why we don't consistently do it.

4. HOW TO INCORPORATE INVESTING IN YOURSELF

Things to consider if you are going to be a champion:

1. You must remove any excuses by incorporating self-investment as a lifestyle, not an event.
2. You must keep your professional skills updated.
3. While we continue to give and pour into others, it is essential that we do not give from an empty cup. We must also ensure we aren't serving or contributing from dated information.
4. You must focus on what strengthens you and practice it.
5. Lack of time, energy, or motivation are no longer excuses to fully invest in strengthening and caring for ourselves. We all get the same amount of time: 24 hours. We must identify and seek those things and events that bring energy. We must surround ourselves with positive, supportive people in an environment that fosters health.
6. Some things drain us and we must not let those things have a prominent place in our lives. Find people and situations that consistently bring inspiration and give you strength.
7. Focus on what brings balance.
8. When we invest in training and exercises that strengthen our spirit and soul, we will have a full, balanced and happier life. When we are balanced, we can serve others better and reap the benefits of success.

God isn't against self improvement. He just doesn't want us to be so focused on ourselves and benefitting ourselves that we forget we are here to serve Him and others. It isn't always about you and you only. Knowing how to invest in you properly helps to ensure we don't become selfish.

As we started this chapter with commitment, we will end with this quote:

"Commitment is an act, not a word."

— JEAN-PAUL SARTRE

Investing in yourself requires you take action daily. Commitment is the fuel to consistency. You must see your commitment to improvement as necessary to reap the benefits you desire. Commit to better yourself. Commit to invest in you and enjoy the benefits of your labor.

10

CHAMPIONS ARE FINISHERS

"And I am certain that God, who began the good work
within you, will continue his work until it is finally
finished on the day when Christ Jesus returns."
Philippians 1:6 (NLT)

IT IS NOT enough to start a project; ensure you finish it. This is the most crucial attribute of champions: they are finishers. Have you started a project, assignment, or job with so much enthusiasm and slowed down by the first obstacle and then stopped short of your goal because you couldn't seem to overcome continual obstacles?

Congratulations, you are not alone and don't you have to stay that way. Champions have obstacles; however, they rise up and fight through them. They put in the work to complete what they started. Let's go back to David in 1 Sam 17:45-50:

"45 David replied to the Philistine, 'You come to me with
sword, spear, and javelin, but I come to you in the
name of the Lord of Heaven's Armies — the God of
the armies of Israel, whom you have defied. 46 Today
the Lord will conquer you, and I will kill you and cut

off your head. And then I will give the dead bodies of
your men to the birds and wild animals, and the
whole world will know that there is a God in Israel!
47 And everyone assembled here will know that the
Lord rescues his people, but not with sword and spear.
This is the Lord's battle, and he will give you to us!' 48
As Goliath moved closer to attack, David quickly ran
out to meet him. 49 Reaching into his shepherd's bag
and taking out a stone, he hurled it with his sling and
hit the Philistine in the forehead. The stone sank in,
and Goliath stumbled and fell face down on the
ground. 50 So David triumphed over the Philistine
with only a sling and a stone, for he had no sword."
(NLT)

After David faced obstacles or distractions from his brother questioning his motives and Saul trying to equipment with equipment that didn't work for him, he went back to the battlefield to confront Goliath and finish him off.

The strength of a person's character is determined by whether they can finish what they started. David finished what he said he would do by killing Goliath and the Philistine armies.

If you are going to have victories and get the praise and rewards like David, you must finish. Employers don't like employees who never finish their tasks. Employees who complete the tasks are more highly valued than those who, though make a valiant effort, fail to complete the project.

Take note of what Jesus says in John 4:34: *"Then Jesus explained, 'My nourishment comes from doing the will of God, who sent me, and from finishing his work."* (NLT)

Wow. His food (nourishment) was in finishing the work of the Father. The Apostle Paul said, *"I have fought the good fight and finished the race that was set."* Not only were Jesus and Paul finishers, but God is a finisher: He finishes what he starts in us.

*"And I am certain that God, who began the good work
within you, will continue his work until it is finally
finished on the day when Christ Jesus returns."*
Philippians 1:6 (NLT)

God wants us to finish, according to 2 Timothy 4:7: *"I have fought the good and worthy and noble fight, I have finished the race, I have kept the faith [firmly guarding the gospel against error]."* (AMP)

The difference between a champion and an average person is that the winner keeps trying when the average person quits. He refuses to consider the possibility of losing because he is convinced that success is imminent. Please adopt the attitude of a champion and don't be afraid to fail. Instead, be afraid of missing opportunities when you don't even try.

Next, people who "finish" know the cost of finishing. Look at the principle Jesus taught about being able to finish:

*"For which of you, desiring to build a tower, does not first
sit down and count the cost, whether he has enough to
complete it? Otherwise, when he has laid a
foundation and is not able to finish, all who see it
begin to mock him, saying, 'This man began to build
and was not able to finish.'" Luke 14:28-30 (ESV)*

If you want to escape embarrassment, you must understand the cost of finishing. Often, people fail because they didn't know the full commitment it would take to finish. For example, they start by underestimating the effort and in the middle of the project or process, they give up and stop because of things they didn't anticipate.

Proper planning helps identify potential problems or situations that will hinder success. If you are going to be a champion, you must plan. There is no way around it. A little planning can stop a lot of pain. If you don't like planning, hire someone. You will benefit in ways you can't imagine.

Finally, finishing can make those around you respect you. Nehemiah is a good example of this. He had mockers and naysayers when he wanted to repair the wall of the city. Throughout the restoration project there were those who mock him, tried to distract him and wanted to destroy him and his mission. But he stayed focus and completed the task:

> "*15 So the wall was completed on the twenty-fifth of Elul,
> in fifty-two days. 16 When all our enemies heard
> about this, all the surrounding nations were afraid
> and lost their self-confidence, because they realized
> that this work had been done with the help of our
> God. Nehemiah 6:15-16 (NIV)*

Notice that when he was finished, his enemies' confidence was destroyed and they were afraid. When you finish, it shuts the mouth of your enemies. All through Nehemiah's efforts of restoring the wall, he had enemies. He stayed focused, however, on his "God assignment." Commitment and focus are hallmarks of a champion when it comes to completing their goal.

Remember, it is important that you know that what you are doing is for the Lord. Nehemiah, the people working with him and his enemies knew it was God that helped them finish. Once you know that, it is easier to commit to the effort and remain focused. If you don't know this, you will get discouraged and forget that, "He that begins the work, will finish it;" you will forget that He has a plan for you, for your good and not for your evil; you will forget what you are doing is for the Lord.

Once you finish the work, you get to enjoy the prize of success. The next and final chapter focuses on the subject of enjoying the reward of success.

11

CHAMPIONS ENJOY THE PRIZE OF SUCCESS

*"Trust in the Lord with all your heart and lean not on
your understanding; in all your ways submit to him,
and he will make your paths straight."* Proverbs
3:5-6 (NIV)

I AM OFTEN INTRIGUED when opponents tell each other what they
are going to do with their prize money. Each of them makes plans on
how they will spend money or go on a vacation, but they are not just
fighting for a heavenly reward, they are looking to enjoy the fruit of
their labor while living on Earth. David did the same thing: he heard
what the King was going to give the one who defeated Goliath in 1
Sam 17: 24-25: *"The Israelites, to a man, fell back when they saw the
giant — petrified. The troops' talk was, 'Have you ever seen anything like
this, this man openly challenging Israel? The man who kills the giant will
have it made. The King will give him a huge reward, offer his daughter as
a bride, and give his entire family a free ride."* (MSG)

Notice here that David was hearing what Goliath was saying, but
more importantly, he listened to what the others were saying. I think
he listened to the words *"huge reward, get the girl or free ride for the
family"* louder than what Goliath was taunting.

For David, this was an excellent incentive package. I can only imagine he wasn't getting this type of deal keeping his dad's sheep. I don't think he got a big reward from his dad for killing a lion and a bear. In his family, he was only a sheepherder and gofer.

1. CHAMPIONS UNDERSTAND THE BENEFITS PACKAGE

Champions fight for more than bragging rights. They fight for a cause. They are fighting to better their lives, the lives of their family, and the lives of others, which is right in sports, work, or whatever cause someone is battling.

If you are going to beat your enemies, know the rewards. There is a reward for breaking habits and having a good attitude; and there is a reward in defeating your enemies. For example, if I stop being late and do the best on my job, sooner or later, I will be labeled dependable and get that raise or bonus. The more value I add, the higher my reward.

The more you learn how to talk and listen to others, the more they notice and the better your reward. The more faithful you are to God, the more you desire him, the better it is for you. The more we please him, the wiser and more blessed we are. We understand that there are rewards, both emotionally and tangible, in serving God.

To the person who pleases Him, God gives wisdom, knowledge, and happiness, but to the sinner, he gives the task of gathering and storing wealth to hand it over to the one who pleases God. This idea, too, is meaningless, chasing after the wind Ecclesiastes 2:26 (NIV).

2. CHAMPIONS UNDERSTAND THERE ARE MULTIPLE BENEFITS IN WINNING

David received a huge blessing when he defeated Goliath and the Philistine army. In exactly the same way, there are prizes, trophies, and accolades to our success. We should learn to receive and enjoy them.

> "18 When David finished talking with Saul, Jonathan
> felt very close to David. He loved David as much as he
> loved himself. 2 Saul kept David with him from that

day on and did not let him go home to his father's
house. 3 Jonathan made an agreement with David,
because he loved David as much as himself. 4 He took
off his coat and gave it to David, along with his
armor, including his sword, bow, and belt. 5 Saul sent
David to fight in different battles, and David was
very successful. Then Saul put David over the soldiers,
which pleased Saul's officers and all the other people."
1 Samuel 18:1-5(NCV)

David got a new home, access to the King, access to the King's family, a blessing from the King's son, a new friend, new clothes, and armed men. Although David wasn't fighting for those things, he reaped the benefits. Yes, unexpected benefits: a new home, a new friend, new clothes, new armor, promotion, and daily access to the King. There are rewards and unexpected benefits when fighting and winning for the "King."

3. CHAMPIONS UNDERSTAND ALL THE BENEFITS ARE NOT REVEALED UNTIL AFTER THE BATTLE

David's fight with Goliath tells us something about God's reward system. That is, God gives us a promise that we can easily identify to position us for more. God's one promise multiplies into numerous victories and rewards. Look at David's numerous rewards from this one battle. In 1 Samuel chapter 18, we can see God's extended blessings to David:

"1 When David finished talking with Saul, Jonathan felt
very close to David. He loved David as much as he
loved himself. 2 Saul kept David with him from that
day on and did not let him go home to his father's
house. 3 Jonathan made an agreement with David,
because he loved David as much as himself. 4 He took
off his coat and gave it to David, along with his
armor, including his sword, bow, and belt.

"5 Saul sent David to fight in different battles, and David
was very successful. Then Saul put David over the
soldiers, which pleased Saul's officers and all the other
people.

"6 After David had killed the Philistine, he and the men
returned home. Women came out from all the towns
of Israel to meet King Saul. They sang songs of joy,
danced, and played tambourines and stringed
instruments.

"7 As they played, they sang, 'Saul has killed thousands of
his enemies, but David has killed tens of thousands.'"
1 Samuel 18:1-7 (NCV)

Look at David's rewards:

- King's daughter
- Free ride for the family
- New living arrangement
- New covenants – from King Saul and his son, Jonathan
- A new friend and the best his friend had to offer
- A Promotion
- New mission - Opportunity to show his skills
- Words of praise - Songs were written about him

In other words, David's rewards were many: a new lifestyle, friend, assignment, praise. He got a new beginning, and when you defeat your giants, you will get a fresh start with endless opportunities for rewards. Defeating Goliath positioned him to be seen by all as to what he could do. It gave access to the King, the King's army, and everything in the Kingdom.

4. CHAMPIONS KNOW THAT ONCE THEY DEFEAT THE FIRST GIANT, THEY ARE REWARDED WITH THE POWER TO DEFEAT MORE

When David defeated Goliath, Saul promoted him to lead a regiment of his army. Through the act of killing Goliath, David was elevated to a position where could encourage and influence those who were once afraid of the Philistine giant. By defeating the giant, it also released the army of God from the bondage of fear that was controlling them.

When you overcome your "giant," everything negative that it was controlling goes down with them. There are people and situations hiding behind the giant, and they get their strength from the giant. But when the giant is out, they are exposed and ready to be defeated. Destroy every enemy in the path of your destiny that the larger enemy or giant controlled and gave strength to. You can do it!

If your giant is lust, stealing, lying, hating, jealousy, anger, rage, alcohol, drugs, etc., focus to kill it and watch how quickly you gain strength to defeat others giants that might be ruling your life. When you destroy those giants, you begin to enjoy earthly rewards within your family, friends, finances, etc. When we work right, we receive God's compensation.

5. CHAMPIONS UNDERSTAND THE PRINCIPLE OF ETERNAL REWARDS

> "8 The women's song upset Saul, and he became very angry. He thought, 'The women say David has killed tens of thousands, but they say I have killed only thousands. The only thing left for him to have is the kingdom!' 9 So Saul watched David closely from then on, because he was jealous." 1 Samuel 18:8-9 (NCV)

David's rewards and excitement from Saul were temporal. They were as good as long as he was in favor with the king. However, we see later in 1 Samuel Chapter 18 Saul getting angry at David because the praises of the women on David were much higher than the praises to Saul. We also find that Saul's anger caused him to try to kill David.

There are lessons we can learn from David's life about eternal rewards:

1. You can be a champion in the eyes of people one day and on the outs the next.

Saul supported David's boldness and courage to defeat Goliath that he even tried to give him his armor. Saul had such confidence in David after he killed Goliath that he kept him in the palace, didn't let him return home, gave him a promotion and full access to the palace. Then jealousy came and David was on the outs.

Is jealousy causing you to be on the outs with someone?

2. You can be a champion in the eyes of one group of people and be despised by another.

Saul was delighted with David when he killed Goliath, but when the women began to give homage to David, he became jealous and started to watch David's every move. Saul started to despise David and entertained the idea that one day David was going to take the kingdom. The thought of David taking over the kingdom overwhelmed Saul with jealousy. It caused Saul to despise David.

Are jealous thoughts causing you to despise someone?

3. You can be a champion praised by the same group, but if you are focused on someone else's praise, you can become jealous.

The women sang praises to both Saul and David. They sang about what they heard went on in battle. There was a count that David received 10,000 kills and Saul killed 1,000. They were singing the testimony of both men.

Saul didn't become jealous because he wasn't praised, he became jealous because someone else's praise was greater than his. The women praised Saul in the same song they wrote about David.

Are you jealous because a group is given testimony about someone that is doing more than you in the same breath that they are praising you?

4. You can be a champion who is loved and hated within the same family or group.

David was invited to the king's house by the king. While Saul began to despise David, his son Jonathan loved David more than he loved his father, Saul. Saul gave David from the king's treasure but Jonathan gave from his heart and gave him personal items. No doubt, Johnthan's items were for royalty and specially made.

Are you finding yourself challenged by receiving love and hate from the same group/family?

5. You can be a champion who helps someone destroy their enemy and the ones you help will try to destroy you.

David helped defeat a number of Saul's enemies, however, when Saul became jealous and angry, he tried to destroy David. Anger and jealousy will cause you to look at things incorrectly. It causes you to look at your friends or allies with contempt and try to destroy them.

Have you found yourself running from those whom you were trying to help because they are trying to destroy you?

These are but a few of the lessons we can learn about David's life as we get a more realistic understanding of the principles of eternal rewards. You might say, "I am lost with how this has anything to do with "eternal rewards."

Well, you have to understand this book is about "attitudes of a champion." When your attitude is "I win," you know that you are living out the promises of God. Look at a number of scriptures that lay out the principles of eternal rewards in light of God's Word.

6. CHAMPIONS UNDERSTAND THE REWARD OF ETERNAL PROTECTION

"3 But the Lord is faithful, and he will strengthen you and protect you from the evil one." 2 Thessolians 3:3 (NIV)

"'No weapon that is formed against you will succeed; And every tongue that rises against you in judgment you will condemn. This [peace, righteousness, security, and triumph over opposition] is the heritage of the servants of the Lord, And this is their vindication from Me,' says the Lord." Isaiah 54:17 (AMP)

"6 Be strong and courageous. Do not be afraid or terrified because of them, for the LORD your God goes with you; he will never leave you nor forsake you." Deuteronomy 34:6 (NIV)

"Discretion will protect you, and understanding will guard you." Proverbs 21:11 (NIV)

"6 Do not forsake wisdom, and she will protect you; love her, and she will watch over you." Proverbs 4:6 (NIV)

"But you will not leave in haste or go in flight; for the Lord will go before you, the God of Israel will be your rear guard." Isaiah 52:12 (NIV)

These are just a few passages that help us understand what eternal rewards provide. We understand what's included in our benefit package and what weapons are in our war chest, knowing that God is our eternal protector. He goes before us and stands behind us as protector. We understand the importance of exercising wisdom when it comes to keeping us protected.

As a champion you have no need to fear your enemy. Protection, eternal protection is yours.

7. CHAMPIONS UNDERSTAND THE REWARD OF ETERNAL INHERITANCE

> *"3 Praise be to the God and Father of our Lord Jesus Christ! In his great mercy he has given us new birth into a living hope through the resurrection of Jesus Christ from the dead, 4 and into an inheritance that can never perish, spoil or fade. This inheritance is kept in heaven for you, 5 who through faith are shielded by God's power until the coming of the salvation that is ready to be revealed in the last time. 6 In all this you greatly rejoice, though now for a little while you may have had to suffer grief in all kinds of trials. 7 These have come so that the proven genuineness of your faith —of greater worth than gold, which perishes even though refined by fire—may result in praise, glory and honor when Jesus Christ is revealed." 1 Peter 1:3-7 (NIV)*

> *"For God so loved the world, that he gave his only begotten Son, that whosoever believeth in him should not perish, but have everlasting life." John 3:16 (KJV)*

> *"15 For this reason Christ is the mediator of a new covenant, that those who are called may receive the promised eternal inheritance — now that he has died as a ransom to set them free from the sins committed under the first covenant." Hebrews 9:15 (NIV)*

> *"13 In whom ye also trusted, after that ye heard the word of truth, the gospel of your salvation: in whom also after that ye believed, ye were sealed with that holy*

Spirit of promise, 14 Which is the earnest of our inheritance until the redemption of the purchased possession, unto the praise of his glory." Ephesians 1:13-14 (KJV)

You, if you are in Christ, and I have an inheritance that cannot be corrupted or denied. If we continue to choose to serve the living God, nothing can stop us from inheriting what God promised. This is a kingdom reward that can't be revoked.

8. CHAMPIONS UNDERSTAND THE REWARD OF CONTINUING TO LIVE GODLY

"3 His divine power has given us everything we need for a godly life through our knowledge of him who called us by his own glory and goodness. 4 Through these he has given us his very great and precious promises, so that through them you may participate in the divine nature, having escaped the corruption in the world caused by evil desires.

"5 For this very reason, make every effort to add to your faith goodness; and to goodness, knowledge; 6 and to knowledge, self-control; and to self-control, perseverance; and to perseverance, godliness; 7 and to godliness, mutual affection; and to mutual affection, love. 8 For if you possess these qualities in increasing measure, they will keep you from being ineffective and unproductive in your knowledge of our Lord Jesus Christ. 9 But whoever does not have them is nearsighted and blind, forgetting that they have been cleansed from their past sins.

"10 Therefore, my brothers and sisters, make every effort to confirm your calling and election. For if you do these

things, you will never stumble, 11 and you will
receive a rich welcome into the eternal kingdom of our
Lord and Savior Jesus Christ." 2 Peter 1:3-11 (NIV)

"30 For we know the God who said, 'Vengeance belongs to
Me—I will repay,' also said, 'The Eternal One will
judge His people.' 31 It is truly a frightening thing to
be on the wrong side of the living God.

'32 Instead, think back to the days after you were first
enlightened and understood who Jesus was: when you
endured all sorts of suffering in the name of the Lord,
33 when people held you up for public scorn and
ridicule, or when they abused your partners and
companions in the faith. 34 Remember how you had
compassion for those in prison and how you cheerfully
accepted the seizure of your possessions, knowing that
you have a far greater and more enduring possession.
35 Remember this, and do not abandon your
confidence, which will lead to rich rewards. 36 Simply
endure, for when you have done as God requires of
you, you will receive the promise." Hebrews 10:30-36
(Voice Bible)

Lastly, God's champions endure because we know we will receive what God promises. We walk in faith believing that whatever God promises. He will deliver. We live not only for promises for tomorrow, but for those that were given and are now manifesting.

Winners enjoy heavenly rewards that encompass God's eternal presence, promises, protection and provision.

We have come to the end of an exciting and spirit-filled experience that entailed learning all about the attitudes that a champion needs to pursue and possess to succeed. Read on to learn different approaches and prompts to take action with all you've discovered.

FINAL WORDS

*"To the person who pleases him, God gives wisdom,
knowledge, and happiness, but to the sinner, he gives
the task of gathering and storing up wealth to hand it
over to the one who pleases God." Ecclesiastes
2:26 (NIV)*

It is incredible to think about all the information and strength we can learn from the Bible if we become intentional about transforming our lives with God's Word. Through this book, you have access to ideas on the attributes of a champion. With the details you're unraveling and applying to your own outlook, you can start living that life NOW!

You can truly maximize this information after reading the book if you combine it with the power of intentionality. When we kick-started this journey together, we juxtaposed the champion Goliath with the champion David. It was evident that, regardless of how the story ended, both of them were champions.

Yet, David was much more intentional about using the knowledge of God to activate his faith in winning. Goliath was intentionally using the wrong things, such as his total reliance on his own might and armor and the army, his previous wins, etc. He died at David's hand because, unlike him, David solely relied on God to give Him victory. David was fully aware of where his strength resided. He acknowledged the power of God within him.

When used the right way in the light of God's truth, the power of intentionality can transform your trajectory. The question now is, "What are you going to do next?" What actionable steps will you take to bring these words you've read here to life and become a champion who portrays the attitudes mentioned in this book?

You cannot afford to become passive with these ideas because, as you can tell thus far, you have so much to gain by adopting these attitudes. So what are you going to do? Here's what you should do: become intentional with absorbing and emulating these attitudes every day. You don't have to wait for a "Goliath situation" before activating the champion within you.

David certainly didn't wait for Goliath as the Bible records in 1 Samuel 17.

I encourage you to read the story about the rest of David's life. You will discover that he had a lot to overcome on the way to becoming king and even after. Throughout his life, we see his total reliance was in God. It didn't matter if he was facing war or human failures, he turned to God to give him victory. You are a Champion. I encourage you to do the same.

Regardless of where you may be right now in life, start preparing to be like a champion just like David by being intentional with how you approach this goal. Have a good heart, ignore critics, and always believe in excellence, even with the smallest tasks. Be intentional with confronting your fears and be willing to pay the price while holding on to your bold confessions.

Always remember that champions are finishers, and this helps them enjoy the prizes of success. Intentionality, with all you've learned, enables you to master the champion's attitude and position yourself at the center of God's will. You have new ideas or may have just been reminded of what you knew. Either way, you have the ideas and resources to get started: what are you waiting for? It all begins now!

You are a Warrior. Greatness is your destiny. Continue to develop the Warrior attitudes that result in your victory in every situation. You win, my friend!

Blessed wishes to you!

"Measure Twice and Cut Once" by Victor J. Coleman, Sr.
Dedicated to my parents, Louis Wilson and Arsola Coleman who both taught me so much in the short time I was with them. They left me with indelible teachings that enabled me to not just survive but to thrive in any environment. Their teachings shaped "The Warrior Within."

Made in the USA
Middletown, DE
27 March 2021